Our Journey to a

God Centered Marriage

Second Edition

Nick and Darlene Nicholas

"What therefore God hath joined together, let no man put asunder."
Matthew 19:6

These words are spoken by the priest or pastor
in traditional wedding vows.

Publication information:

Our Journey to a God Centered Marriage
Second Edition

ISBN: 978-1-998014-35-4
Copyright © 2025 Nick and Darlene Nicholas

Print Editing and Layout and e-pub creation:
I. Gaudet, Success Publications

Published by:
Success Publications
Box 10, Egremont, AB T0A 0Z0
www.SuccessPublications.ca

Table of Contents

NOTE:

You will note that there are 2 different font types used in this book. This is done deliberately as there are 2 voices – that of Nick, and that of Darlene. This is a deliberate choice by the authors.

Nick's voice and writing are in this font.

Darlene's voice and writing are in this font.

Chapter 1
The Ceremony

The sun was shining brightly, there was a warm breeze blowing in off the lake and the chapel was small and cozy. As I stood with my best man and the Navy Chaplain, all of us in our dress uniforms, my anticipation was off the chart and my pulse rate must have been peaked out.

As I looked down the aisle of the chapel, I was completely overwhelmed with a deep, deep sense of love as my beautiful Darlene started walking toward me on her father's arm. That was the day that we were married by man's law, repeated our vows, and the Chaplain said these words, *"What therefore God hath joined together, let no man put asunder."* (Matthew 19:6) In reality, God had joined out souls in marriage three years earlier.

As I now look back on that beautiful day over forty-four years ago, I can see how God's presence in our marriage has not only kept our relationship loving and strong, but it has also galvanized us into an unbeatable team as we dealt with the many difficult challenges life has poured on us.

We're going to share with you what we've learned over those years and how we came to embrace God's love, how He became the center of our marriage, and how we accepted His strength and guidance to weather those storms.

There are some basic things that we need to understand upfront. When two people come together in a relationship they each bring all of their past with them. I like to think of it in terms of showing up with two bags, one with my belongings and the other with all of my baggage from my past life. Secondly, a marriage does not mean that either person is going to stop being an individual, even though they have been joined as one in marriage. We must each be allowed to be ourselves while at the same time honoring our union. Learning what this means and learning how to practice it can be a significant challenge. Realize that, in any relationship, one of the individuals will gravitate to being the dominant member. I don't like the connotation of the word dominant regarding a relationship as it tends to indicate that one spouse is dominant and the other is submissive. I much prefer the term, "person in charge." What we have learned in our years together is that the in-charge role must be shared, by that I mean that neither person is constantly the one in charge. Issues must be discussed and solved as a team not directed by one person, unless it is an urgent situation and must be acted upon immediately. Darlene and I have adopted a practice we call kitchen table conferences. I'll discuss this in more detail later.

One final point you need to know. This is Darlene's first book and that my writing style is to share my message through stories. What we are about to share is the story of the journey we have taken to have a long, strong and loving marriage. Finally, all I share is from experience, what I learned from a Christian Psychologist, what I've learned from standing in God's beautiful light when I was twelve seconds from death and what Darlene has experienced in her life. Please realize there are many, many books on marriage relationships and hundreds of marriage counselors and pastors who are very good at what they share. What we share is our perspective and not to be considered the only way. Understand it doesn't happen because of the marriage ceremony, it takes work, patience, and more than love. Oh yes, love is critical but since it is an emotion, it will wax and wane due to the challenges we encounter. Darlene and I have learned that along with love there are other critical factors: friendship, trust, and just liking each other. Without these necessary ingredients, marriage can be like traveling a rocky road. I can speak from experience as these two ingredients were not present in my previous two marriages. Our greatest prayer is that what we share with you will help you to experience a wonderful and beautiful God centered marriage.

Chapter 2
How do we live in the presence of God and become God centered

I read my daily devotional each day, and one morning as I was reading, this message stood out to me.

You do not realize that you would have broken down under the weight of your cares but for the renewing time with Me. It is not what I say, it is I Myself. It is not the hearing Me so much as the being in My presence. The strengthening and curative powers of this you cannot know. Such knowledge is beyond your human reckoning.

This would cure the poor sick world, if every day each soul, or group of souls, waited before Me. Remember, that you must never fail to keep this time apart with Me. Gradually you will be transformed, physically, mentally, spiritually, into My likeness. All who see you, or contact with you will be, by this intercourse with you, brought near to Me, and gradually the influence will spread.

You are making one spot of earth a Holy Place, and though you must work and spend yourself ceaselessly because that is for the present your appointed task, yet the greatest work you can do, and are doing, is done in this time apart with Me. Are you understanding that?

Do you know that every thought, every activity, every prayer, every longing of the day is gathered up and offered to Me, now. Oh Joy, that I am with you. For this I came to earth, to lead man back to spirit-converse with his God.

To me, the two most important messages in this reading are:

1. Living in God's presence has enormous strengthening and healing powers.

2. When we live in God's presence consistently, we will, over time, be changed physically, mentally, and spiritually into His image. Others will see those changes and ask how to achieve the same change.

In the 1980's Johnny Lee recorded the song, Looking for Love. Here are the words to the chorus:

I was lookin' for love in all the wrong places
Lookin' for love in too many faces
Searchin' their eyes
Lookin' for traces of what I'm dreaming of
Hoping to find a friend and a lover
I'll bless the day I discover another heart
Lookin' for love

It's a great song. I recommend that you listen to it. The reason I shared this chorus is because it so accurately speaks to what happened in my life when I met Darlene and began my real journey back to God. I was looking for a true love in my life and also a love that would fill the deep void I felt in my soul. We've spoken a lot about our love for each other and how that love is grounded in God's spirit of love. So, I want to talk about looking for the love that gives us fulfillment in our soul.

I often hear people say that they strive to grow closer to God but aren't sure what that means, or how it can be accomplished. We've all heard priests and pastors speak on this, giving us their interpretation of the knowledge from the Bible. Please don't misunderstand me, the interpretation of the Bible by our clergy, and honestly by ourselves, is critical in our spiritual growth. However, since my near-death experience, (NDE) and my deep relationship with God, I have gained a deeper understanding of the Bible's message. I understand now that there is an intellectual interpretation and a spiritual interpretation. Let me give you an example. Our interpretation of the crucifixion and resurrection is primarily focused on the fact that Christ died on the cross to give us forgiveness for our sins. That is absolutely a correct intellectual interpretation. However, the spiritual message goes much, much deeper. I'll go in more specifics in the chapter on forgiveness, but for now, suffice to say that one of the deeper meanings is this. As Jesus hung from the cross, He looked out at his tormentors, those who had tortured Him nearly to the point of death and then nailed Him to the cross to die. Yet, he called out to His Father, *"Father, forgive them for they know not what they do."* The spiritual message is that no matter how badly we are treated, betrayed, insulted, or beaten, we must still forgive. What this means is that we are forgiving the person, not condoning the action. This is critical to our spiritual growth and growing closer to God. Failure to do so leaves a darkness in our spirits.

The love that fulfills the soul is not found in the temporal world. It can only be found in the spiritual world. Let me explain what I mean by sharing how I came to know this.

Two weeks after being engulfed by God's beautiful light, I awoke. As I lay in the twilight between being asleep and awake, I saw the light. I wasn't in the light; I just saw it as a bright strobe came directly into my heart. At that moment, I experienced the most overwhelming understanding and deep belief of who God is. God is a superior positive energy force of pure love. Yes, God is energy. In fact, He shared this when Moses asked, *"Whom shall I tell the people You are?"* God replied, *"I am that I am,"* meaning that He can change into any form He chooses.

Scientists will tell you that energy cannot be created or destroyed and can only change form. Our spirit is both positive and negative energy.

God is the positive energy in our spirit while Satan's fear is the negative energy in our spirit. Since our spirit is energy, it can only change between fear and love.

What does this mean as we search for soul fulfilling love? It means that soul fulfilling love already resides within us through God's spirit which already lives in our spirit. To find it and grow it, we must first learn how to manage our spirit. The reality is that we can determine whether our spirit is controlled by Satan's fear or God's love. The more our spirit is controlled by God's love, the closer we grow to God. We'll go into this in more detail a little later.

Let me explain how I have come to understand and believe it since that wonderful awakening morning. As we have our first heartbeat, while still in our mother's womb, God is placing His spirit into us, his spirit of pure love. Don't confuse this with the Holy Spirit, which will come later in our lives, as we profess our belief and our acceptance of Jesus as our Lord and Savior. With that first heartbeat, we have been created in God's image, the image of pure love. As humans, we are our spirit, not our body or mind. The body and mind have their separate functions as directed by our spirit. As we experience Satan's fear, the negative side of our spirit appears. I'll explain that in more detail in the chapter on fear. Our spirit is now made up of both fear and love. Who we are is defined by which side of our spirit is in control of our life. We can either be seen as a loving and kind person, or a mean-spirited person. God gave us right of free choice, which means choosing to make our decisions from His spirt of love, or from Satan's spirit of fear. Again, it is important to understand that we are our spirit, the body and mind have other functions as directed by our spirit.

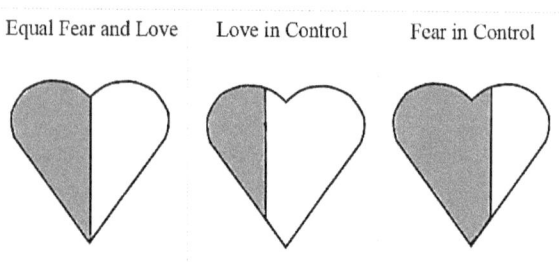

Equal Fear and Love   Love in Control   Fear in Control

Let me give you a visual. Imagine your heart as we depict it on Valentine's Day. Now draw a line vertically dividing it into the left side and right side. Now, lightly shade in the left side. What you are seeing is an example of your spirit. The bright side is God's spirit of love; the shaded side is Satan's spirit of fear. To make it easier to understand note that we refer to our spirit as our emotion of love or fear. Okay, now draw a line just left of the center line and erase the shading. What you are seeing is an example of a positive thought converting fear energy into God's spirit of love. Now, draw a line just to the right of the center line and shade everything to the left of the line. What you are seeing is the conversion of God's spirit of love into Satan's energy of fear.

Here is the amazing thing… every thought you have moves that center line either right or left. So, it is through learning to manage our thoughts that we live in God's presence, the spirit of His love living within us. I will explain how to manage your thoughts in the chapter on fear.

When that center line is predominantly and consistently left of the center line, we are living in God's presence, the degree to which that is true depends on how far that line is left of center. Be aware that it will never eliminate the shaded area as fear is energy and cannot be destroyed, there is no such thing as being fearless. The true meaning of fearlessness is that God controls most of our spirit and our life, and we completely trust Him to guide us and protect us. When this happens, we face fear with a determination, strength, and courage that can only come from God.

I also want to address the message of healing, and people seeing and feeling a difference when they are around you. Here is a personal example. On a Sunday morning in 2024, I felt as if I was coming down with a cold. I took my Zicam that Sunday and again on Monday. By Tuesday afternoon, I felt horrible. Darlene took me to the local Mercy clinic where they tested me for Covid-19. The result was that I had what they called the A-Flu. By that time, my temperature had risen to 102 degrees. They called Mercy hospital and arranged for my admittance. At seven that evening, I was in my room. It was the Tuesday of the State of the Union message, and I wanted to watch it. I only made it through the first thirty minutes before I was out cold.

I remember nothing that went on around me until Thursday morning; I woke up feeling as though I had never been sick. The nurse came in and was surprised to see me sitting up. She left and returned shortly thereafter with the doctor. The doctor's first words were, "You are my miracle."

I was confused as I didn't consider myself a miracle, I just knew that I felt good. She went on to explain what happened. On Wednesday morning she'd come in to see me and after checking my fever, x-rays of my lungs, and taking into consideration my age, she didn't believe that I was going to make it until morning. However, she said, "As I started to leave, I turned and looked at you and I realized that you were different, I didn't know how or why but I knew you were different. Once I realized this, I knew I had to save you. I immediately knew what I

16

needed to do, and it was different than I would have done for anyone else. The nurse was a little surprised but carried out my orders."

I then shared with her what happened to me while I was out of it. Sometime during that time, I felt myself slipping away. I knew I was dying. I said "God, nine years ago, I stood in Your wonderful light and received Your mission for me. I've been doing that mission for nine years, I know I can't come home until it is finished. Does this mean my mission is finished and I can come home? I'm ready, or are You going to intervene?"

That is the last I remember until Thursday morning. The doctor looked at me, smiled and said, "I guess you just answered my question as to why you are different. I'm also a very spiritual person and I know that God has guided my medical career and has used me to heal the sick. This, however, is the first time His using me is so evident." She also asked me why I didn't consider it a miracle.

I responded, "When we have a deep spiritual relationship, this is what He does for us. He has a mission for all of us, and we cannot go home until that mission is complete."

The nurse, who had stood quietly listening to our conversation, asked me how that can be since people die very young, and often babies don't live long enough to leave the hospital. Sadly, they didn't live long enough to have a mission. "That's a great question," I told her. The real answer is way above my pay grade, but I would surmise that the child's mission was to put the parents into a situation that would direct their decisions to cause their actions to move them closer to God's plan for them.

As the devotional passage said, living in God's presence consistently has strong healing powers and will eventually transform us, physically, mentally, and spiritually into His image, and that means our spirit is consistently controlled by God's spirit of love. Also, that transformation will be seen by others, and they will want to know why.

That event was another turning point in our lives. That was in March of 2024 and in August of 2024 I published my last book, <u>My Life Reclaimed by the Grace of God</u>. That event was also the foreshadowing of God's further mission for Darlene and me as a couple in the writing of this book. Remember, God is always with you. Please take some quiet time with Him and listen for the thought that will show you your next step along His path for you.

Chapter 3
My journey to that
life changing October day

As I said, we show up to a new relationship with two bags; one with our personal belongings and the second bag contains everything (our memories and actions) that we've collected in life, up to that day. I'm going to share what I brought to that wonderful day and then Darlene will do the same.

I'd grown up in a Christian home and been taught a strong work ethic, to respect people, and to be optimistic and forward thinking. Most importantly, I had acquired a deep faith and a love of Jesus. From my pastors and Sunday school teachers, I'd learned that if you lived by God's laws, and followed the golden rule, bad things would not happen to you. If you were to experience bad things, that meant that you had failed that law and God was punishing, you.

This was the life I lived for my first sixteen years. In the summer between my junior and senior year of high school, it all changed. Beginning that sad June day in 1958, when my mom passed away, I was, in my opinion, brutally betrayed three times in a span of a few years. This is what happened and how I felt about it.

It was in June of that year that my mom died after a botched surgery. I was holding her hand and praying for God to make her well and let her come home with us. At that moment, she opened her eyes, squeezed my hand, looked at me, smiled and took her last breath. Through my devastation and tears, I asked God what had I done wrong that He was punishing me?

A short five weeks later, I learned that the girl I had been dating through most of high school, and had seriously considered marrying after graduation, was dating four of my friends behind my back. I simply looked upward and said, "God that is strike two."

I went off to college in the fall of 1959 with a brand-new attitude; to hell with right or wrong, if it feels good then just do it. After my freshman year, I dropped out of school and married my first wife, whom I'd met in college. We'd been married for eight and a half years when I discovered she was having an affair with my best friend. I looked upward and said, "God that is strike three. I don't need You in my life if this is how You are going to treat me."

Between the spring of 1968 and October of 1980, I rebelled. I spent time as a homeless person until a cold November day, the 22nd to be exact. On that cold November of 1968, I stumbled into an Army Recruiting office, hungover and looking to get warm and some coffee. Yes, I also found a new direction in life as a member of the U.S. Army. Like any young GI, I spent my duty time training hard and working hard. My personal time was spent drinking, chasing women, and generally going wild. Two years later, June 1970, I married for a second time. My years in the Army went well, however, my marriage not so much.

Then on Monday, the 20th of October 1980, my whole world totally changed. I was assigned to temporary duty (TDY) to Ft Benjiman Harrison, IN. I was there training Captains to be commanders of Recruiting Companies. I was being billeted in a local motel, as base housing was not available. On that fateful Monday morning, I was having breakfast with several other NCO's and as I looked up, I saw her, a beautiful strawberry-blond, in uniform, walking towards our table. I looked at her and said to myself, 'that is my next conquest'. Little did I know then how wrong I was, and how meeting her would cause a seismic shift and change both of our lives forever.

On Wednesday evening, I went into the lounge to get a beer. Two NCOs that I knew were sitting in a booth with two women, and they invited me to join them. One of the women was the beautiful strawberry blond. As I sat down next to her, a shock went between us. It felt like a shock from a light socket. The guys sitting across from us said "What was that? We saw it all the way over here!"

I invited her back to my room to continue our conversation knowing I was going to make my move. I gave it my best effort, and she shut me down hard. I made my second attempt, and she very clearly let me know that no meant no. We spent the rest of the evening talking. I didn't know why, but I opened up to her and told her things I'd never told another living human being.

We became dear friends and, yes, eventually we became lovers. Later, we realized that God had joined our souls in marriage when we were shocked. In a perfect world, my second wife and I would have gotten an amicable divorce, and Darlene and I would have gotten married by man's law and lived happily ever after. The world isn't perfect. Soon, all hell broke loose, and for three years it rained down on us.

Chapter 4
Darlene's journey to that
life changing October day

It was October of 1980, and I was working as the Assistant Operations NCO at the Second Recruiting Brigade in Atlanta, GA. My job was working with the guidance counselors in 13 cities to ensure the recruiting numbers were correct. I felt that it was important to attend the guidance counselor course to have a greater understanding of their job and give me some credibility with those that I worked with. I felt that I needed that because I was not a recruiter, I was admin. I was approved to attend the class in Ft Benjamin Harrison, for 20 Oct 80. I was excited, so I packed my car for a two-week temporary duty assignment (TDY) to Ft. Ben Harrison, IN. I arrived on the 19th and checked into my motel, The Howard Johnson, located just off base. My class was to be conducted at the motel because there was a lot of activity on base and there was no training space available.

Monday morning, I went to the restaurant to get my day started. I saw one of my guidance counselors already at a table, so I headed over to join him. There were two other soldiers at the table that I did not know. One of them was getting ready to head for Ft Ben as he was also on temporary assignment. He was gracious and let me have his seat. I believe I thanked him and then joined into conversation with MSG King. I had a lot to learn since I was not a recruiter. That evening, I was in my room with my roommate and one of my classmates. He was going over some of the material we had covered in class that day to help me understand it better. The NCO that had given me his chair that morning stopped by my classmate's room to drop off a carton of cigarettes that my study mate had asked him to get at the PX. Just a blip in the study season.

On Tuesday evening, we had game six of the World Series between the Kansas City Royals and the Philadelphia Phillies on, I was doing a study session, and the nice NCO came in briefly. On Wednesday evening, my roommate and I were in the bar having drinks with some of our classmates. Next thing I know is that nice NCO joined us at the table. He slid into the booth next to me and when our elbows touched, we each experienced an electrical shock. I finally got to meet him, and we started to converse. He had been in the restaurant with a friend, and he stopped in the lounge to get a drink and never went back to the restaurant. I was enjoying my conversation with Nick, yes, I finally found out his first name and he invited me back to his room to keep talking. Well, I was up for more talk, but he had other things in mind. Guys, you know what he was thinking. Me, on the other hand, had made a commitment to myself to not get involved in a relationship with anyone as I was only here for two weeks. I was not in a relationship with anyone at the time, and a temporary relationship was not in the books for me. Nick was trying very hard, but I said "No."

We had a long conversation, and he told me things that he had never talked about with anyone else. I told him a lot about me too. I told him why I was not in the mindset to have a fling. I had gone on active duty in 1977 because I was in a catch 22 position, no job – no car, no car – no job. I left my boyfriend at the time to improve my financial position. I returned home after being away for six months, driving my new car and wanting to surprise him, but I was the one who was surprised, and got a broken heart to boot. I was badly hurt, so it became my "mantra" to not become involved with a married man. I wanted Nick to try to make things work with his wife when his temporary assignment was over.

We became friends and spent our off time together. During my second week at Ft. Ben, my heart had become involved, so I did not end up being true to my desire not to have a fling. As I was packing up to return to Atlanta, I told Nick I was not going to be the one to destroy his marriage. So, I left to go home, and Nick and I had decided not to contact one another again. That didn't last too long though. Nick called me and we each confessed our love for each other.

For the rest of his temporary assignment to Ft. Ben, I went to visit him once, and he came to Atlanta to visit me once. I always felt that I would not get involved with a married man, but I knew, deep in my bones, that Nick and I belonged together. We had a lot of "white water" ahead in our relationship, not internally, but caused by external forces. Our so-called friends did things to try and hurt our relationship. God kept us strong and eventually, we won. God is what makes our relationship work. We believe that He joined us in marriage that day when the electric shock occurred, but it took three years to make our marriage legal in man's world.

God gives us challenges, and I believe it is how we deal with those challenges that makes us stronger. My love for Nick has been forged in fire because of my experiences. I may get frustrated with things, but my love is stronger. I know we will survive until it is time for us to "go home to God."

Chapter 5
Why are decisions so important to us

You now have an idea of some of the baggage that Darlene and I each brought into our marriage. Thankfully, on that night in my motel room, we set the foundation for open communication that has been such a critical part of our marriage.

We were friends first, thus allowing our love to make us strong.

For a marriage to be stable, long lasting and God centered, all these issues must be brought out and discussed, and, in some way, be resolved. Otherwise, totally open communication is damaged. Frankly, without fully open communication, the foundation of trust is compromised, and trust is critical to a long-lasting relationship. However, to openly communicate, we must make a committed decision to be open and honest.

As I said, all decisions are made emotionally first and we then find some quote, "logical justification." We must understand that no action is taken without it being motivated by emotion.

It is important that I share with you, at this point, that what we refer to as emotions are, in reality, our spirit. I learned this after I stood in the light. I'll explain more later but suffice to say here that our spirit of love is God's spirit alive within us, and the spirit of fear is Satan's weapon. He uses it to blind us to God's love and guidance. Therefore, know that all decisions are made spiritually: God's spirit of love, or Satan's spirit of fear.

Sadly, we have had limited training in decision-making. Don't misunderstand me, I know there is training on how to gather all the facts, explore the outcomes, consider the risks, and evaluate the consequences. I taught these techniques for years. As important as this knowledge is, it doesn't explain how decisions are motivated and then made.

You may be wondering why this discussion is even necessary in a book on a God centered marriage. The simple answer is that everything we do requires a decision. The type of marriage we are going to have is determined by the decisions we make, decisions made independently by each party. Now you can better understand why each person's belief and spiritual relationship with God is so important. It will be that belief and relationship that will guide their decisions throughout the marriage.

So, how are decisions really made? I'm going to share with you in the next chapter what I've learned through my life experience over the last eighty-two years, what I have learned from my Christian psychologist, who I refer to as coach, and to what I've come to understand after standing in the light.

A quick side note. I had my near-death experience (NDE) in December of 2015. Since that day, I've been constantly and regularly gaining new understandings of things which I'd never previously had any knowledge. I'll not go into a deep detail here as to how it came about, and how it has affected my life, over the past nine plus years as I spelled it out in detail in my previous book, <u>My Life Reclaimed by the Grace of God</u>.

Chapter 6
The process of decision making

Our five senses: touch, taste, smell, hearing, and sight are our connection to the world around us, the temporal world. What those senses do is gather information and that information generates a thought. For example, you see a very attractive person of the opposite sex and have a positive thought. That thought, in turn, generates a feeling which is attached to one of your emotions. For example, that positive thought gives you a good feeling and that good feeling is attached to the emotion of love, God's spirit. That emotion, in turn, motivates an action, since it is motivated by God's spirit it will be a positive action which is appropriate for the situation.

Here is where it gets interesting. Everything we encounter, through our senses, causes our mind to interpret what we are sensing as either positive or negative. This determination is based on our current situation and what we have encountered in our experience. Think of it as a glass half full or half empty, as everything has two sides. It can be good or bad depending on how we perceive it. Frankly, much of the time, it's good or bad because we label it that way again based on the current situation and our experience. This, of course, is a simplified explanation. If you want a much deeper understanding, you'll need to contact someone with a PhD in psychology or similar credentials.

With that understanding, let's look at how it plays out in relationships. For example, a man and a woman meet at work, immediately their senses engage. He is sensing, she is pretty, has a very nice body, is pleasant to talk to and she really smells good. I'd like to give her a whirl. She senses that he is quite handsome, tall, and muscular. He is easy to talk to, seems quite intelligent, has a good job and would probably be a good provider. I could do a lot worse. If you want to learn more about the difference in how men and women perceive each other, please read the great book, <u>Men are from Mars, Women are from Venus</u>.

When a couple meet and are having these thoughts, they experience a physical reaction as well. If they really connect in that meeting, that feeling is positive and can be construed as love, lust, or like. If they don't, then what they see are the negative thoughts. I've heard it said that the man is thinking, "Let's find a place," while she must have a reason. Granted, this is an oversimplification, but you get the idea.

The decision to marry is a very important decision, and there are many motivators; the euphoric feeling is interpreted as love but is that

31

love intellectual or spiritual? The decision can be intellectually motivated by many things like lust, financial considerations, peer pressure, societal norms, family pressure, status, and the list goes on. Of course, in the best scenario, actual spiritual love is the desired motivator. Each of the scenarios I pointed out are, in fact, intellectual decisions motivated by the emotion of fear, yes, even lust, it could be the fear of having missed out on something you physically want. Let me apply these to the three marriages I've had so you can see the reality of what I mean.

I married for the first time when I was only eighteen and she was seventeen. My motivation was that I was lonely, I'd been betrayed, and I needed my 'man card' back. Frankly, I felt unwanted, and that really scared me, and yes, my hormones were running wild. I identified the euphoric feeling as love when, in fact, the feeling was, let's get real here, it was restoring me as a winner rather than a loser, and it demonstrated that I was worthwhile. We connected intellectually and physically, but not so much spiritually. All marital relationships do have some level of spiritual love, unfortunately it is not the controlling reason for the decision to marry. Please understand that this does not rule out the possibility that as they are together over time spiritual love can grow and become the foundation of the marriage. In my first marriage that never happened to my knowledge. However, even after we divorced there was still some level of love that remained.

When I married the second time, I'd been running hard for several years. Skirt chasing and heavy drinking was beginning to have a major effect on my physical and emotional wellbeing and I was afraid that if I didn't settle down, I'd end up in the hospital, plus my Midwest upbring and my previous religious belief dictated that I should be in a family relationship, (societal, religious, and social pressure). I'd known her for a while, and I thought we got along well. She seemed well grounded. I wasn't sure it was love, but I was convinced that over time, the deep relationship would come. We see how well that worked out. From her perspective, she was divorced with three children and looking for security. The euphoric feeling lasted for three days after the marriage. From that point on, it was disaster waiting to happen.

My marriage to Darlene was completely different. I had no intention of finding another wife. My intention was to have a good one-night stand with a beautiful woman. Thank God she squashed that idea very quickly. What was different was that instead of throwing her out as I normally would have, I felt the need to trust and open up to her and get to know her as a person, which, in my opinion, is critical in a long-lasting relationship. What was most important was that we both came from the same spiritual base. Yes, trust God, He really does know what He is doing, even though His ways often seem mysterious to us.

As you look at the three real life relationships, do you see the major difference? The first two were made from fear, and we did not share the same level of belief in God. My relationship with Darlene was put together by God. The spiritual base was there. Think about it! Was it a coincidence that we were both TDY at the same time, to the same place, and were staying in the same motel? I learned in my special ops training that there is no such thing as coincidence. Everything happens for a reason, and everything has a purpose. Our meeting was not coincidence; it was God directed. There is a great country song Keeper of the Stars by Tracy Byrd, that speaks to this. One of the lines from the song is very prophetic when it comes to God centered marriages. It goes like this, *"Someone had a hand in it long before we ever knew, the keeper of the stars."*

You're probably saying something like that sounds very nice and romantic, but how do I know if this is the right person? That, my friends, is a great question. Let me try to explain. God has a plan for every one of us, and a mission for every one of us. We plan our lives on what we want and desire, but when it differs from God's plan, He gives us a course correction. This happens through something that happens in our life. Usually, it is something that we are not really happy with. He has someone for each of us, and when the time is right, He will bring them into your life, usually when you least expect it and are not looking for them.

The simplest way I can explain it is that you'll know in your heart that this is the person God has planned for you. Darlene said it perfectly in chapter four when she said, "Deep in my bones I knew that Nick and I belonged together." Why this happens is way above our ability to understand, only God understands. As we say in the military, it's way above my pay grade. Live your life based on a strong belief and relationship with God and do the best you can based on each situation. Will you stumble and make mistakes? For sure. This is not a bad thing though, because this is how we learn. When we have learned what we need to know to follow God's plan, He will put the right person there. Don't worry about it, don't try to manipulate it, just let God handle it. He's smart and won't let you down.

For my take on it being God's plan, my MOS (military operations specialty) was 71L40, or Administrative Specialist. The class I went to take was for the MOS of 00R40, or Field Recruiter. As far as I know, I am the only non 00R to attend the Guidance Counselor course. I wanted to attend it to make my work with those Guidance Counselor's I dealt with telephonically better. My boss could have easily sent me to the local MEPS station (Military Enlistment Processing) to spend a day with a Guidance Counselor, but that didn't happen. Take into consideration, the rest of the 'coincidences' such as time and place, I whole heartedly agree God was behind it.

Chapter 7
Preparing for God's plan

Patience had never been one of my strong traits. Frankly, I think that is true of many people. I grew up in the 40's and 50's when it was a much slower and laid-back time. We hadn't yet discovered the internet, cell phones, YouTube and other instant methods of communication. We didn't have a Keurig to make our coffee; we had to wait for it to perk. We didn't have microwaves and had to wait for the oven to cook the food. We had not yet been introduced to twenty-four a day news channels and had to wait for the evening paper or the six o'clock news. Several years before any of these things came about, an event took place that significantly increased our desire for immediate gratification. I'm not saying it was necessarily bad; however, it foreshadowed what was to come.

Does the name Ray Kroc ring a bell with anyone? It should, because he was the man who bought, some say stole, the idea from the McDonald brothers. They had a small hamburger stand in San Bernadino, California and turned it into a worldwide operation we know today as McDonalds, Mickie D's or the golden arches. It of course affords fast service, burgers, fries, drive-up windows, and much more. After that our lives began to change. Where families used to sit down together for a meal and enjoy a nice conversation, suddenly they were able to stop at McDonalds, grab a burger, fries, and drink for less than twenty-five cents and be on their way. From that point on, Americans began to deeply embrace instant gratification. Patience was no longer necessary, at least if we were hungry. Today, we impatiently wait for the few minutes it takes for our microwave to nuke a frozen dinner. We no longer need to wait for the newspaper or the six o'clock news, we just whip our out-cell phone and pull up the latest news. Sadly, it is often posted before the facts are in, and we are misinformed.

Because of our newfound ability to receive instant gratification, we often find ourselves applying that same standard to our relationship with God and in our marriages. We raise up a prayer to God and then expect something to happen immediately. The truth is that God has a long-term plan for each of us. Try as we will to do things in our time, everything in our life is going to be in God's time. We run our lives on our time schedule however, in God's kingdom, there is no time, it is eternity. I never really understood this until I was blessed with a near death experience and was embraced by His beautiful, overwhelming love and peace.

The doctor told me that with my heart malfunction, from the time it started to death was thirty-two seconds and my pacemaker brought me out of it at twenty seconds. He said I was only in the light for twenty seconds. However, I knew I was in it for a lot longer than that. Yes, there is no sense of time on the other side.

In marriage today, we want what we want when we want it. Sadly, all of this, and other changes in our world, seem to have us living in a "me" generation. In a God centered marriage, we must be ourselves as individuals, but at the same time be respectful, understanding, compassionate, and caring about our relationship as a couple. Darlene and I, like everyone else, went through the struggles to learn how to live this way. As the following chapters roll out you will understand what I mean. Suffice to say, let God guide and direct you in this endeavor.

I share all of that with you to point out that, in God's time, we will find the soulmate He has for us, and in His time, we will be prepared to fulfill the mission He has for us as individuals, and as a couple. Let me give you an example of what I mean by being prepared to move to the next level.

Pretend you are in high school again and studying calculus. One morning, a college professor comes in to teach the class. He is teaching calculus as if his students are college juniors. It is highly unlikely that you will understand half of what he is teaching because you aren't prepared to understand calculus at that level. There is still much you need to learn first.

We must prepare for everything in our lives. That includes becoming God centered and preparing for a God centered marriage and to be able to accomplish God's mission for us. That preparation can be lengthy and even painful. If you've ever been in the military, you know exactly what I mean. Preparing to be able to accomplish the military's mission is long, hard, and painful. Always remember, however, that all the crap life dumps on you is not God's punishment, as I used to believe. It is His preparation for your mission.

I'll always remember when I entered the army, I weighed one hundred twenty-five pounds and couldn't do ten pushups. Ten long weeks later I weighed one hundred and eight pounds, had less than eight percent body fat and could do one hundred pushups on each hand and run for ten miles without breathing hard. I was proud, fit, and strong. Did it hurt? Damn right it did. Did I ever want to quit? Yes, I did but each time I had a drill sergeant right on top of me driving me on. I had to work at growing stronger and I've since learned that if we want a deep relationship with God, we must work for it. We must have the courage to keep going when there seems to be no end to our pain in sight. I'll tell you that the hard work and pain I felt to achieve success in the army and the hard work and pain I experienced on my journey back to God, both gave me rewards beyond anything you can imagine.

Darlene and I have experienced the same hard work and pain to achieve the wonderful marriage we have. We never considered quitting but there were times when the future looked bleak. Instead of it being a drill sergeant driving us on, it was God, who is at the center of our marriage that drove us on to a beautiful reward.

Before God joined Darlene and I in October 1980, He had prepared us for our meeting with all that happened in all the years prior. Once we were joined, He began to prepare us for the mission He had for us as individuals, and as a couple. In the Bible, we see examples of how God prepared those who were to carry His message to the world, even before they were introduced to Jesus. Afterwards, He continued to prepare them to accomplish His mission for them and withstand all the evil resistance they would face. Frankly, that preparation can be very painful and often requires suffering through many extremely difficult challenges. It is through this preparation that we learn how to turn to Him for the strength, resolve, courage and faith to achieve our mission and to weather the constant resistance we receive from others who do not yet have the necessary understanding to fully commit to His plan for them.

You've heard little about my prior life experience before meeting Nick. Here is more insight into why I was so committed to Nick and my love for him. I was the youngest of three children. Even though I grew up with two sisters, I would have to say, I felt like an only child. My dad was always working, and when I was around him, I felt that he had little patience for me. My mother was always there, in the home, up until I was 16. I would say the use of the word "mother" is the formal address for her. We never called her "mom." To me, the word "mom" means love. Anyway, she found work outside the home. My relationship with my parents was nothing like that of the few friends I had. I know my parents loved me, but I felt that they didn't know how to show it. I was starving for love and acceptance while growing up. I wanted to feel deeply and truly loved and accepted for who I was. At school, I was made fun of. At home, and at school, I felt like I was always the brunt of the joke and was often laughed at. I always said I had more fingers on one hand, then I had friends. Two of those were real friends, and I'm still in touch with them 50 years later.

It was this deep desire for acceptance and a truly deep and committed love that galvanized my commitment to never settle for less from my life partner. Over the years, I experienced relationships that ultimately proved to be rather superficial. As I said earlier, when I met Nick, I was not looking for a relationship as I'd just left a relationship that ended in infidelity on his part.

This journey was long and painful. However, in retrospect I now realize, as Nick said, it was not punishment, but rather preparation for the wonderful God centered marriage Nick and I have today.

As I spent time around Nick, I began to realize that the love I felt from him was deep and true. I was so convinced that it was true, I encouraged him to go home and try to make his marriage work. Looking back, I now realize that it was God who gave me the strength to let Nick go so he could save his marriage, even though I knew in my heart that we would be together. What Nick said about God having a plan for all of us is so true, and over the years we have accomplished so much as a team. Truth be told, our love grows stronger every day.

Little did Darlene and I realize at the time that all the very difficult challenges we struggled with were strengthening us in so many ways as individuals and as a couple. Preparation God's way is not easy and requires that we persevere when things seem impossible and to learn from the experience. There were many things we needed to learn. In the following chapters, we're going to share what we needed to learn and how He guided us in that learning. One great learning I will share now is that when there seems to be no way, God will provide a way.

Have you ever noticed that you experience the same thing repeatedly? It might be God challenging you to change something, and until you change, the repeating happens again and again. I just wanted to be loved, and I had too many superficial relationships looking for that love that did not work. So, I made the decision to stop looking, and what happened? I met Nick. I broke the cycle and things worked out for me. The cycle can be hard to break, but it can be done. Instead of looking for love, we need to let love find us. It is God that places that love in your life. Be patient and know it will happen in God's time.

Chapter 8
Our preparation begins

It is impossible to have a fully God centered marriage without total and complete honest communication. This is one of the most difficult things for us to learn, and even harder to practice.

In my years as a professional speaker, consultant and trainer, the problem I was asked to address the most was how to improve communication. Corporations lose millions of dollars each year because of missed or misunderstood communication. Families also struggle with this same issue. Marriages fail because of lack of communication. I've been asked again and again why it's so hard, and how do we fix it?

The answer does not lie entirely with the tools we use to communicate. First, we must understand that our interpersonal messages are communicated in three ways simultaneously. The words we use (verbal 7%), strictly intellectual; our voice tone (vocal 38%), a combination of intellectual and emotional; and our body language (visual 55%), strictly emotional. What makes it even harder to understand is that sender and receiver both send and receive those messages through their own filters. Those filters are, in fact, made up of things like our age, our education, our gender, our race, where we're from, and all the baggage we've accumulated over our lives. The use of text, email, and social media only communicate verbally. So, it is easy to see why messages are often misunderstood. Even so, that is not the greatest deterrent to completely open and honest communication. No, fear is the number one deterrent to honest open communication. I've discussed this in detail in my first Christian book, <u>Reclaiming My Life -- My Journey Back to God</u>. However, it is so critical in a God centered marriage I want to review it here.

One of our basic instincts is to belong, to be accepted by others, and yes, to be admired by others. We all hold back those things that we don't want others to know about us, so we hide those things away and live in fear that they will somehow leak out. I have referred to this as our vulnerability vault. It is a place in our minds that we shove those negative things and lock them away. We then expend enormous energy guarding them, always fearful they will leak out and expose our mistakes and bad decisions. That energy is negative spiritual energy, Satan's weapon. It is the negative side of our spirit and has a major impact on how we live and how we communicate. Since we don't want to slip up and let it out, it leaves a permanent part of our spirit that stays negative.

We respond to questions from one of three levels: auto response which ensures we don't reveal what's hidden, thinking (intellectual) response to ensure we give safe facts without revealing what's hidden, and feeling (emotional) response where we open up and give the full truth. Unless we communicate from the feeling level, complete communication cannot exist.

If you're not sure of this, think back to the last time you went to the doctor so sick you could hardly sit up. It seems the doctor always breezes into the room in high spirits and asks, "So how are you feeling?", I'll bet your response was fine or something like that. That is your auto response. Remember, never show weakness. Then he asks you to tell him/her what your symptoms are and to explain how you feel. Explaining your symptoms requires you to think before you answer. When you answer the question, "How do you feel?", you report from the feeling level and the truth comes out.

On that night in October of 1980, talking to Darlene, I would have normally given an auto response and told her to leave. But she seemed so open, honest, and sincerely cared, I had to stop and think for a second, her attitude and presence made me feel safe. These feelings of safety and the feeling she wasn't judgmental overwhelmed me, and I opened up. What if I'd gone with the auto response? Well, God was not going to let that happen. I've learned that God communicates with us through our thoughts and feelings. This was validated by Betty J Eddy in her book, <u>Embraced by the Light</u>, sharing her second near death experience. She said she communicated with Jesus, but not with words. She had a thought, and the answer came back to her as a thought. This is important for us to understand, as God guides us through our positive thoughts and positive feelings. Our negative thoughts engage our fear emotion and Satan is motivating our decisions.

Since I had made the decision to "stop looking" I believe that I was able to be open to hearing what Nick was telling me about his life. I wasn't in "Self-protection mode". I felt safe because I was not looking to be involved in a relationship, and I didn't feel Nick was pushing for one. As he said, my safe feeling gave him the same feeling of safety, and he felt comfortable sharing with me.

In March of 1981, I was in a horrible place. My then wife and I were constantly fighting, and I was seriously considering divorce but didn't have the courage to pull the trigger and file. I didn't want the pain and hassle of a divorce, but I didn't want to be in the marriage I was in. What a dilemma. I was in a highly stressful army recruiting assignment. Everyone I worked with thought I was a spy for a one-star General who was investigating recruiter malpractice, and my true love was a thousand miles away. To make it worse, I'd not yet learned to fully trust women and to understand the depth of Darlene's love for me. On that cold miserable Monday morning, just outside of Ft. Devens, I emotionally crashed. It was at that point that I only wanted to die. Then I heard a soft voice telling me to get help. That got me started to work my way back from the emotional abyss and changed my life forever. I now realize that the soft voice I heard was a thought that God placed in my mind.

Yes, it's true, you must hit bottom before you can start to rebuild yourself and achieve your full potential. It was Sir Isaac Newton who proved that for every action there is an equal and opposite reaction. What this means in our life is that as low as we go is as high as we will rise. When we hit rock bottom and there is no lower place to go, then we have the potential to rebound extremely high. A great example of this is John Travolta. He started his movie career in 1974, but his first big movie success, <u>Saturday Night Fever</u>, came quickly and easily. After that, every role he played was a success. Then it all changed. He fell from grace so to speak. Then in 1996, he starred in the movie <u>Michael</u> the story of an archangel. Later, he was on the late-night show and was asked about his comeback. His response spoke volumes about how he saw life. He told the host that in the beginning he was at the top of his game, but that in life you must pay your dues. He went on to say that he was a success before he paid his dues and that he had to pay his dues before he could star in <u>Micheal</u>. In my case, I had to hit rock bottom before I could truly start my journey to where I am today. When the time is right, God will guide you through this traumatic experience and guide you through a meaningful course correction. I tend to be stubborn, so He had to hit me in the head with a two by four to get my attention, but it worked.

One of the first books my special forces counselor had me read was, <u>Why am I Afraid to Tell You Who I Really Am</u>, written by John Powell, a Jesuit Priest. It is focused on self-disclosure and why we are afraid to reveal our true self. Regardless of your current situation, I strongly recommend you read this book.

Sadly, one of the ways we protect those negative things is to tell a little white lie, or even a big lie. Unfortunately, we forget which lie we told to whom, then it gets even more stressful.

Going back to that first night, Darlene and I talked in the motel, I emptied a good portion of my vulnerability vault to her. Why, may you ask?

What is the secret of letting it all out? It is a deep feeling of trust and a safe space where you have no fear of being judged or ridiculed for your missteps. I must emphasize that no matter how egregious your sins and mistakes may have been, God still loves you and will forgive you, and like the prodigal He will welcome you into His loving arms and celebrate your return. Always remember Jesus died on the cross to forgive our sins. Believe me, if He was willing to forgive me for my many horrible deeds, He will certainly forgive you. However, to accept that forgiveness, we must learn to forgive ourselves. I'll address that in more detail in a later chapter. Why did I have such trust in Darlene? I certainly didn't trust anyone, especially women, at that point in my life. I must say that the trust I gave Darlene at that time was limited. I trusted she would listen and not ridicule or judge me. I trusted her like you would trust a counselor. The trust I gave her, even though limited, was given to me by God. There can be no other explanation.

The first step in clearing our vulnerability vault and being able to communicate openly and honestly is to find someone whom you trust and will not be judgmental or ridicule you. The best places to look for this is a good psychologist, preferably a Christian, or a good faith-based life coach. I must warn you that all of the garbage will not come out at the same time. Some is buried so deeply you've forgotten it, or you have lied about it for so long, you now accept the lie as truth.

Let me give you a personal example. In 1969 I washed out of flight school. I was so embarrassed I had let so many people down that I couldn't share the real reason, so I made up this little story. I told everyone that I experienced a hard landing and messed up one of Uncle Sams helicopters, and they decided to wash me out. Many years later, in a session with my Christian coach, the truth came out. Darlene was with me that day and somehow the discussion was about my past career. I blurted out the truth without thinking. The truth was that I had a panic attack while flying solo at 1500 feet. Believe me, that's not a great situation to be in. I disregarded all protocols and flew right through the aircraft in the landing pattern without looking. Only by God's grace did I not kill myself and several others. Of course, that truth, I believed, showed my weakness. When I finished, Darlene looked at me with her mouth open. That's not what you've told me for years she said. You see, I'd told that lie for so long, it became my truth. Understand that our vulnerability vault is layered, and it takes time for each layer to make its way to the surface. Think of it as peeling an onion, yes it stinks, brings tears to your eyes, and must be dismantled one layer at a time.

The great news is that as the layers are removed, your positive spirit of love grows, and your negative spirit of fear diminishes. This is because you have just converted a lot of negative spiritual fear energy to God's positive love energy. The result is that you are now closer to God and He has more control of your spirit and that has a very positive effect on every decision you make. Yes, I started the task of peeling the onion with the help of my Special Forces counselor, but I still had a long way to go. Once Darlene got to Ft. Sheriden, she worked hard to help me move forward but I know that my slow progress really frustrated her.

After I got transferred to Ft. Sheriden to be with Nick, I would occasionally flare up and my anger and frustration would come out. He never reacted or came back to argue. This was even more frustrating, as it kept happening. I don't remember what it was that I flared about, but one day, Nick came back and said, "You piss me off." I immediately laughed out loud and said, "Thank goodness." You may be wondering why I did that? You must have some comeback to all these flares of temper that I was having and when you don't get it, what is happening to the person you are flaring with? They just take it and take it until they finally have enough. All those times that I was flaring, I believe, and Nick will tell you from his side, that he was stuffing it down. That is when we finally started to "communicate," and my flares decreased in occurrence.

She just gave you a great example of failure to be fully honest in our communication and one way to break the cycle. Why did I withhold the truth? Again, fear. This wasn't like what happened in Indiana, that was like the first layer of the onion. This was deeper down and would reveal what I perceived as a weakness, an inability to be vulnerable. You see, my previous life experience taught me that if I shared my true feelings, I'd pay a heavy price.

As the words left my mouth, I knew I was going to pay for it. But instead, she laughed and said, "It's about time." She wasn't offended because she gave me permission to be myself. What Darlene did was just one more way that God worked through her to help me to get my life on a positive path. Do we have arguments and disagreements? Sure, we do, because we are human. Fortunately, however, coach taught us how to argue without damaging the relationship. We'll cover that in a later chapter. Thank you, sweetheart, thank you coach, and thank you God.

Chapter 9
Houston, we have a problem

What Darlene and I were hoping for was that our friends would support us, that my divorce would be amicable, and that somehow the army would assign us together. Did that happen? Oh no, in fact, all hell broke loose. Many of our friends turned against us, and some even tried to destroy us. My divorce became a three-year ordeal, and the army reassigned me to the Boston recruiting battalion.

So much for a rousing approval of our relationship... not. Why so much resistance if, in fact, it was a relationship put together by God you may ask? We didn't realize it then, but we've learned since, that anytime you try to live a God centered life, and work to grow spiritually as you get closer to God, Satan will be coming after you hard. If you do not get resistance, then you are probably not doing what God wants you to do. When this happens, don't stop, but simply say, "God, I'm not sure what to do here. Please give me your guidance and strength."

I shared this with a priest one day, he looked at me and said, "Nick, it can't be that simple."

I replied, "Yes it can Father, Darlene and I do it all the time and it works every time."

Darlene was already in a good place spiritually in her relationship with God. I, however, had a different story. Satan came after her by putting her through the struggle of a long-distance relationship and putting temptations in front of her. What Satan did to me was much different and could have been a major threat to our future. Unfortunately, at this point, I was still struggling with trust, both for Darlene and for God.

Chapter 10
Our road to Heaven
had to pass through Hell

When my TDY was over, I returned to the Kansas City recruiting battalion as a nurse recruiter. I hadn't been back for two weeks when it happened. Again, it was a Monday. I had just gotten to my desk when the battalion commander called me and said that General Connely, the deputy commander of United States Army Recruiting Command (USAREC) was on the line on for me. General Connely was heading up a massive investigation into recruiter malpractice. No recruiter, in his or her right mind, wanted that man to even know their name, let alone to get a personal call from him.

I didn't know what to expect when I picked up the phone and I was shaking in my boots. "Good morning, sir," I said.

"Good morning, Sarge," he replied, and got straight to the point. He hit with a rhetorical question. "How would you like to be reassigned to the Boston Recruiting battalion as commander of the Lowell, MA recruiting station?" At that time Lowell station was the second largest station in the command.

"Well, sir, I'd rather come to the headquarters and be on the training team." What I heard next froze me in place.

"I need you in Boston within a week. Good luck and safe travel." Click. Once I got my composure, I stumbled through the rest of the day starting preparations for moving to Boston. Later that evening I called Darlene and shared the devastating news.

That evening Nick called and told me he was being reassigned to Boston as a station commander. He sounded like someone had just stolen his dog. I knew it was not what we planned, but I knew that God intended for us to be together, and everything would work out. I told him that I knew he would do a great job and not worry. I just knew we were destined to be together, and we'd make it.

When I got off the phone, my spirits lifted. God, what did I ever do to deserve this wonderful woman. I was getting a masters lesson in what true love really means.

Ten days later, I was in my recruiting station in downtown Lowell, MA being introduced to the outgoing station commander and the nine recruiters by the company first sergeant. The tension was great, but like the brigade Command

Sergeant Major (CSM) and the battalion Sergeant Major, they also believed I was there as a spy for General Connely. Afterwards, as I sat in my office, I had a humorous thought. It was something that a fellow NCO friend of mine said one day when things went haywire. "So, Mrs. Lincoln, other than the assassination, how was the theater?" Sometimes gallows' humor can lighten things up. The next sixteen months were some of the most difficult and stressful of my career.

My second wife insisted on going with me, and the arguments and discord grew worse now that she knew I was in love with someone else. This was certainly something to be expected, and if the situation were reversed, I'd probably act the same way. Sadly, it only added stress to an already difficult situation.

My drinking increased. I was drinking two or three six packs an evening, and on weekends, I added some quality whiskey, yes, brother Jack, last name Daniels. The pressure from the battalion leadership was excruciating and the tension at the recruiting station only added to my misery.

I then remembered what one of my ops training drill sergeants told me when I hit the wall and fell to the ground. He kicked me and said, "If you're breathing maggot, you're alive, so on your feet and keep moving. There are no victims in this man's army." From then on, that was my driving motto. No one was going to make me their victim. Today, Darlene and I refuse to be victims. We will find a way to persevere. My entire attitude changed, and I took charge. Unfortunately, even with our best intentions, life still wears us down.

On a cold and nasty March morning in 1981, I was on my way from Ft. Devens to Lowell, only about 25 or 30 miles. I hit the wall, and I crashed emotionally. I pulled off to the side of the road, beat my head on the steering wheel shouting, "I can't do this anymore!" over and over. I then collapsed in the front seat and sobbed. I wanted to die. If I'd had the means, I'd have ended it right there. Then I heard a voice telling me to get help. I began to calm down and regain my composure. Again, it was time to get on my feet and move forward.

I'm Catholic, so I went to see the priest. After I shared all my woes, he looked over his half-rimmed glasses and said, "Your life is so screwed up. I can't help you, but I know who can," and proceeded to pick up the phone. Wow, did he really have a direct line to God? No, he didn't but he convinced a counselor at the Special Forces Stress center, who counseled 10th Special Forces soldiers when they came back from a mission, to work with me.

It was my first real step forward. I worked with him from March of 1981 until May of 1982. I finally won the trust and respect of my recruiters, certainly not the battalion leadership, and our production improved significantly.

I usually got to the station early to do my paperwork and plan the day. Shortly after, one of my NCO's would come in make the coffee. I was working away when I noticed a pair of shiny shoes in my doorway. Without looking up I said, "Don't just stand there sarge, get the coffee started." Then I heard a loud clearing of the throat. As I looked up, I was looking into the face of Major General Maxwell Thurman, the Commanding General of the Recruiting Command. He was often referred to as "Mad Max," by both NCO's and officers. Of course, not to his face. He was rightly feared by many, and I'd just called him Sarge and told him to get the coffee started. It wasn't starting to be one of my better days.

I snapped to attention and welcomed him to my station. He was smiling and said, "Sit down Sarge. I'm here to talk about your next assignment. I'm bringing you to the Headquarters to work with our JOIN (Joint Optical Information Network) team. I need you there as soon as possible." A week later, I was in my new assignment. Yes, the leadership in Boston couldn't get rid of me fast enough. They did take the time to destroy me on my efficiency report, hoping to destroy my career. I didn't realize it, then but my career soon began to flourish after that. I guess it's true, he who laughs last laughs longest.

From the night that Nick called me in January of 1981 to tell me about his reassignment, until we were finally together at Ft Sheridan in June of 1983, it was a very stressful time for both of us. We talked every night and shared our love and discussed what was happening in each of our daily lives. He, of course, was going through a living hell, and it finally caused him to literally hit the wall. I wanted to be there with him but that wasn't possible. However, in our daily conversations he shared what was happening with the Special Forces Counselor and I gave him all the support and love possible from long distance. I shared some of what I faced but I didn't want to add to his stress. I knew that I was not going to do anything to jeopardize our loving relationship, and these struggles simply made my love stronger.

A female friend of mine, who I used to go out partying with before I met Nick, kept pushing me to go partying with her. She tried to convince me that I should go on dating because I was crazy to be true to a married man with a real history of cheating. She thought I was setting myself up for a big hurt. But I knew better because I knew God had destined us to be together. This was the strongest love I'd ever experienced, and I knew Nick felt the same way.

I managed one trip to Boston during that time. Then he came to Atlanta for the fourth of July and again on Christmas. That year, we started a tradition which we still practice. We bought a Christmas ornament with the year on it. I know long distance relationships are very fragile and often fail, but I didn't look at our relationship as a long-distance relationship. I looked at it as a purposeful journey to a loving destination.

Then I got the call for which we had been waiting for so long. General Thurman was transferring Nick to USAREC Headquarters in Chicago, IL. This meant that we were getting closer to being together full-time. It also looked like his divorce was progressing to conclusion. Yes, God was rewarding our patience and faithful struggle.

Nick's new assignment was to conduct briefings and demonstrations of the new computerized sales system which the army wanted to deploy in every recruiting station. For that time, it was a revolutionary idea. But I'll let him tell you more about that. In June of 1983 I was reassigned to the IT division at USAREC Headquarters. From the time he was reassigned to USAREC, until I arrived, I made two trips to see him, and he came to see me once or twice. We were starting to see light at the end of the tunnel.

Chapter 11
Together again

In 1964, Buck Owens sang the hit song, <u>Together Again</u>. Here are the words to the first verse and the chorus.

"Together again my tears have stopped falling,
the long, lonely nights are now at an end.
The key to my heart you hold in your hand
and nothing else matters,
we're together again."

The song, of course, was about a couple who had been separated and were now back together. The situation for Darlene and I was different, but also somewhat the same. The couple in the song had separated because of a problem. For us it was a forced separation, and now we were together again. We had been in a long-distance relationship for over two years and now we were together again.

It's said that living with someone day to day is a lot different than dating and spending short times together. Because this is when the warts start to show their ugly head. Toilet seat left up, dirty socks on the floor, you snore, and when did you pick up that annoying habit? Yes, the euphoria of the love that is shared is often challenged by life's everyday issues.

I know that our religions teach us that living together before marriage is a sin. I won't disagree with that; however, I believe there are exceptions. My question would be how we define marriage? Frankly, in my opinion there are two different definitions of marriage. The first, and in my opinion the most important one is, God joining two people's souls in marriage. The second, of course, is the joining of two people on paper in accordance with man's law. Don't misunderstand me, I'm not disrespecting marriage by man's law. My point is that, if over fifty percent of marriages today fail within the first ten years is fact, then that tells me that marriages not put together by God, often struggle to be sustained long term. Of course, that doesn't mean that there aren't those that do survive but I guess the question is, at what cost?

Earlier, I spoke about my first two marriages, and even though feelings of love were present, we were joined by man's law, not God's law. Darlene and I will always believe God did in fact join our spirits in marriage on that wonderful day in October of 1980. Today we celebrate our spiritual marriage anniversary and our wedding day anniversary in July 1983.

Wait a minute, you may be thinking, are you saying that if I don't have that type of experience, God did not join us in marriage? No, not at all.

Each person and each marriage are like a flake of snow, completely different and unique. There has never been one just like it and there will never be another one just like it. You will experience your own individual unique epiphany of God's joining your souls. I wish I could tell you how it will happen, but that is way, way above my pay grade, and is a moment reserved for you and God. Suffice to say, you will both know when it happens, and believe me, it is a feeling such as you have never experienced. Be patient, wait for it, don't try to manipulate those feelings of perceived love to justify your actual motivation for marriage. If you do, it's a disaster looking for a time and place to happen. Believe me, I've been there, and the pain can be excruciating.

Chapter 12
Settling into the routine of daily life

Dating is exciting, the wedding is awesome, and the honeymoon is euphoric. Ours was a wonderful week in the Wisconsin Dells. Back home now, so what's next? It's back to the everyday grind of work and handling problems. Of course, for the first few months, maybe even a year, while the marriage is still new and fresh, it is still pretty great. But then the burdens of everyday life start to take the bloom off the rose.

As time goes on, the daily routine begins to weigh on the marriage. Sometimes you must work late. Sometimes the work environment can be very frustrating. Suddenly, it seems there is no time for working on keeping your marriage fresh. Sadly, all too often, we find ourselves taking our frustrations out on our loving spouse. Everyday life is constantly dumping crap on us. Often, money is tight, and you find that you can't do the things you did when you were single. You start to feel the pressure of working long hours, paying bills, running errands, and the list goes on. Now you and your spouse are arguing over little things, and the blaming and finger pointing starts. Unfortunately, over time, you each begin to live in your own world, and the distance between you grows. Frankly, this is just life. Believe me

Darlene and I were not immune; we do not live in a fantasy world. We are just like you, we struggle with the everyday crap, face many challenges and must work through them like everyone else. However, because of our deep spiritual love and our relationship with God, He gives us the strength and guidance to persevere and live a life of peace and love.

I know that sometimes it seems that no matter how hard we try, life just keeps hammering away. Sounds grim, doesn't it? The good news is that it doesn't need to be that way. Don't misunderstand, life is not going to back off and leave you alone. Your work colleagues and your circle of friends, who may love you to death, are not going to go out of their way to fix things for you. Let's face it, they have their own problems.

So then, what is the answer to having a long happy marriage? It's hard work, shared love, compassion, forgiveness, and, of course, a strong relationship with God. That's right, all too often after marriage, we become complacent in focusing on our relationship. Of course we must focus on our work, daily challenges, and a myriad of other issues.

The fact is we must establish our life priorities. I would ask you to consider your priorities. Life can be complicated because it is made up of so many different moving parts. So, we must decide what is most important. It is not going to just be one thing, it is many. Sit and quietly consider this and make a list of things in your life that are important to you and your spouse then prioritize them and keep those priorities in mind as you plan your day. It looks simple enough on paper, doesn't it? But as they say in sports, the team looks like the winner on paper, but the game must be played on the grass. The same is true of life. It must be lived every day, and we must always find ways to work through the issues and obstacles that life brings.

The key is to do it together as a team and have God as the third member of the team. That means talk to each other and as a team ask God for His guidance. Believe me, His solutions are far better than ours. For Darlene and me, our priorities look like this; God, country, relationship, profession, and everything else falls after that. Often, profession is considered the number one priority. I guess it could make sense because we must have the money to take care of our family and life's expenses. Unfortunately, we only have so much energy and if the majority of that is spent on making money, we have little energy left to expend on more important things.

My brother, bless his soul, never made more than 25,000 in any year his entire life. People would raze him about not trying to do better. I loved his response. He would just smile and say, "Well, I never saw a hearse with a full luggage rack pull up to an ATM on its way to the cemetery. You can't take it with you, so I don't make it a big priority in my life." Pretty wise guy, I think.

In order to live our priorities and be a team, there are things that we must be able to do to be successful. We must learn to communicate, as I shared earlier. Since there will always be disagreements, we must learn a healthy way to argue so that it does not damage the relationship. We need to learn to be a couple, and at the same time, maintain our individuality. We all make mistakes and do things that hurt our spouse, so we must learn to forgive. And most of all, we must learn how to put God at the center of our existence. The next chapters will be devoted to each of these.

I'm not trying to paint a dark picture of married life. I'm only sharing what I've experienced, and what I've seen in relationships. But when God is at the center of the relationship, all the crap that threatens your love and marriage is so much grist for the mill to be used to strengthen your love and resilience. So, as I said, it needn't be this way. Unfortunately, unlike your car, relationships and marriages don't come with an instruction manual.

What Darlene and I want to share in the following chapters is what we've learned in our over forty-four years of marriage. What we are sharing has served us well. Have our lives been all roses and unicorns? Heavens no. We face challenges just like you. Even today, as we reach our senior years, I'm eighty-two and she is seventy-one, we still face life's brutal challenges. Remember, our spiritual battle goes on every day of our lives until God calls home. This is how we grow stronger spiritually, which was the first mission God gave to each of us at birth.

Chapter 13
Trust God

Let me share a story with you. Many years ago, when I was still doing training and consulting with fortune five hundred companies, I experienced, what I believe, is a good example of putting God first. By that I mean, letting God direct your decisions. I was working with a mid-level executive. He had just received a memo from his boss outlining what the CEO had directed on a particular situation. His approval was required.

Unfortunately, he did not agree with the directive, in fact, it was counter to his Christian beliefs. He looked at me and said, "Nick, I don't know what to do. I cannot, in good conscience, give my approval of this, but if I don't, I could lose my job, and I can't afford that. I have a family and a mortgage to pay."

I suggested that he should share it with his wife that evening and for the two of them to say this prayer. "Father, we are faced with this very difficult problem, and we do not know what to do. Please show us the direction we should take and give us the strength to follow Your will, to You, we pray." Then wait quietly and the answer will come to you.

Sometime later, I was again working with him and here is what he told me. "My wife and I did as you suggested and after a very short time, we agreed that we should disapprove of the directive. We believed that no matter what happened, God would give us the guidance to handle whatever happened. Somehow, we would find a way to handle it." Then he smiled and told me the rest of the story. After his disapproval, all hell broke loose. His boss reamed him out; he received a memo from the head office to reconsider his decision or face dismissal. He refused and was given one week to turn his projects over to his replacement and clean out his desk.

Less than a week later, he received a call from a friend, who was with a competing company, and was offered a position higher than his present one, and for a significantly higher salary. Often, in the heat of everyday life, we forget that God oversees everything.

You may be saying, "Wow, that was a gutsy move! I don't know if I could take that kind of risk." I fully understand what you're saying but let me share what I mean when I say God is in charge and will not let you down. This is it; Man plans, and God laughs. It's not really funny but it sure is true. We make our plans and often times they don't work. When they don't, that is God telling us that the plan we had is not in line with his plan for us. When this happens don't despair, sit quietly and give God a chance to give you direction through a thought. Here is an example where Darlene and I experienced what I'm referring to.

In 2010 my dad passed away. Darlene and I had been his financial support and his medical care takers at cost of between thirty and forty thousand dollars a year. It was time to take care of us. We decided to shut down my company and stop traveling. Unfortunately, the financial crash of the real estate market at that time was devastating to us. We went from having over two hundred thousand in equity in our home to being upside down fifty thousand dollars. We had intended to use some of that equity to make it through the next year, but that opportunity was now gone. We tried everything we could think of to fix it, but it all failed. So, we sat at our kitchen table holding hands and prayed this prayer, *"Father, we are in a lot of trouble and do not know what to do. All of our efforts have failed. As we sit here tonight, we are putting it into Your hands. We know that You are by our sides at all times, so we ask that You show us what You want us to do. In Jesus name we pray."*

Within a few minutes Darlene said, "Since it's Christmas time lets go to Arizona and visit my folks."

Wow, that was certainly not the answer we expected but we did it anyway. It turned out to be a major change of direction in our lives that brought us closer to where we are today. You'll learn more about that in later chapters.

The Bible gives us an even greater example. Adam and Eve were living in the paradise God created for them. His only conditions were that they love Him, trust Him, and not eat from the tree of knowledge. They were tempted to disobey God's three simple requests, and we know how that worked out. He is no different today than He was then, even though the situation is reversed. We are living in a sinful and chaotic world, but He promises us His Kingdom, a paradise, if we will but do three things, love Him, trust Him, and do not fall prey to the fear and false promises which Satan forces on us every day. I know it sounds like a monumental task, and it does require deep faith and belief, but it is the difference between a life of happiness with a clear conscience and a life controlled by fear.

I recently read something in my daily devotional that I believe puts a sharp point of this story.

"*Just go step by step. My will shall be revealed as you go. You will never cease to be thankful for this time when you felt at peace and trust and yet had no human security.*

"When human support, or material help of any kind is removed, then My power can become operative. I cannot teach a man to walk who is trusting to a crutch. Away with your crutch, and My power shall so invigorate you that you shall indeed walk on to victory. Never limit My power. It is limitless."

As I shared earlier, when Darlene and I met, my relationship with God was basically nonexistent. Thank God hers was very strong. For us to have a God centered marriage I needed to reestablish my relationship with God. How did I do that and why was it so hard? It was by Darlene's patience, love, and support, and by God's Grace, even though, at that time, I'd not yet come to understand how God was working within me.

Just before I met Nick, I had decided to "stop looking" for a man to complete my life. That was a big reason why Nick's advances to me didn't work. I just felt this way and I had to trust my instincts which I believe was God saying, "slow down." I am not a church going Christian. I am a God loving Christian with a strong spiritual relationship with God. What do I mean by this? There are so many religions for us to select from. Each one has their own doctrine. I'm sorry, but I don't believe that many of them hold closely with what God really wants. In my mind, churches today speak to what their congregation wants to hear. Why? Because sadly, religion is too much like a business and it seems their focus is on making enough money to sustain their doctrine. I prefer to live my life the way I believe God directs me, and as you read our book, I hope you will see that it is working for me. God is the final arbitrator of my life after all, and I will only answer to Him. So, the bottom line for me is, I treat others the way I want to be treated, and I trust God.

Chapter 14
Reconnecting to God

When I first met Darlene, I was anything but religious, as I was spiritually and morally bankrupt. It's not easy to admit that publicly, but I've found you can't grow spiritually and morally until you openly admit where you are in life, and that you, and only you, are responsible for where you are. Others are not responsible for how you react or respond to what they say or do. It was your decisions that got you here. Think about it. When you plan a road trip, you must know where you're starting from before you can design a route to your destination.

My special forces counselor did not treat me with kid gloves. In fact, he was harder on me than any drill sergeant I'd ever had. That was good because as I said earlier, sometimes we just need to be hit between the eyes with a two by four to get our attention. He forced me to look at my actions and made me take ownership. You do not coddle war fighters, you challenge them. Yes, when you are in the place I was, you point the finger at someone else and you blame others for your failures. In short, you justify your actions with the belief that you are a victim. There is no place for this type of attitude in the U.S. Army, and there certainly is no place in our lives if we are to develop and maintain a strong relationship with God.

Why, you may ask, am I bringing this up in a book on a God centered marriage? It's simple really, because when things get difficult in life, or in a marriage, we often tend to point fingers and blame our job, our spouse and anything else that we can think of. We start telling ourselves that we are victims of other people's actions, and we start to believe they are all conspiring against us. What that really means is that we have convinced ourselves that it was the actions of others that caused us to be in this situation, and we are not responsible in any way.

Sadly, victims are not willing to accept responsibility for their position in life. Since others are responsible for their situation, then others should be responsible for fixing the situation. We see a lot of that today as many people look to the government to fix their lives. Sadly, they expect someone else, or the government, to fix things for them. Besides, it was the government or other people's fault in the first place. Folks, it doesn't work that way, it is the decisions we make based on our perception of situations created by others.

As in the example I gave you about the real estate collapse, we didn't cause it, but unlike many others, we didn't turn to the government for a handout and expect them to fix it. No, only someone with a victim mentality does that. We knew we needed do decide what was going to happen in our life, of course, with God's guidance.

I think you can see why understanding this is so important in a lasting relationship. In a God centered marriage there is no place for victims, both spouses must be able to accept responsibility for their actions as individuals and as a couple and be willing to work with each other to solve any issue. Selfishness and self-centeredness are a cancer in the marriage and will, in time, kill it. In our opinion, it is necessary to put each other first while honoring our own individualism.

When I hit my emotional wall on that day in March 1981, I had also hit the bottom. All the finger pointing and blaming others for my situation lost all its validity. I was forced to face the cold hard reality that I, and I alone, was fully responsible for my position in life. I had reached a point where I was at the bottom and the only way forward was up. That meant that my only option was to stop wallowing in my own misery, self-pity and victimhood. I got me here, now it was my responsibility to work my way back to morality and a spiritual relationship with God, and to once again be like that young boy living in a Christian home in Kansas so many years ago.

Chapter 15
Two tear drops

In 1999 Steve Wariner sang a sad but beautiful song entitled, <u>Two Teardrops</u>. Here are some of the lyrics:

Two tear drops floatin' down the river
One teardrop said to the other
I'm from the soft blue eyes of a woman in love
I'm a tear of joy that she couldn't carry
She was so happy she had just gotten married
I was on her cheek when she wiped me away
*   with her glove*
I could tell by the look in her eye she didn't
*   need me*
So, I drifted on down and caught a ride to the
*   sea*

The other tear said we've got a connection
I'm a tear of sorrow born of rejection
I'm from the sad brown eyes of her old flame
She told him they'd be lifelong companions
Left him with questions and not many answers
I was on his cheek as he stood there calling
*   her name*
I could tell he had a lot of my friends for
*   company*
So, I drifted on down and caught a ride to the
*   sea*

This is a great metaphor for where we were when Darlene and I met. Any tears she shed would be tears of joy, born of her strong relationship and love for God. I, on the other hand, would be shedding tears of sorrow for a life of rejection, and a rejection of God.

You are probably scratching your head wondering how could you and Darlene ever have a God centered relationship and marriage when only one of you embraced God's love? That is a great question, but think about it, aren't there many couples who have different levels of spiritual relationships who find themselves in similar circumstances?

Here are a few things you need to consider when evaluating your faith and belief in God. First, God resides within each and every one of us as He made us in His image, His spirit of love. Secondly, there are two kinds of faith and belief, intellectual and spiritual.

Many years ago, I was talking with my priest, and I said to him, "I'm going to say something that I don't believe you will agree with. I believe that over eighty percent of parishioners are intellectual rather than spiritual believers."

He came back with, "Nick, you are right, I don't agree with you. I believe the number is more like ninety-five percent." To me, that was shocking coming from a priest.

Let me explain to make it more understandable. As I said earlier, our senses generate intellectual thoughts which we commit to intellectual beliefs. Here is an example; you witness a minor fender bender accident. Based on what you saw, you develop an intellectual belief of what happened. But when the police interview all witnesses there are two other people who believe it happened differently. You now are faced with standing by your belief or wavering because what you just heard makes good sense.

Here is how the priest said it, "During the service, most everyone is attentive and shows signs of acceptance of the word. As they leave church, they shake my hand, smile, and tell me that they really got a lot out of my homily. Then I look in the parking lot and see them cutting each other off to get to the exit as quickly as possible."

Here's how I understand it. While in the church service, their senses generated intellectual thoughts of how God, through Jesus, is there to care for them and they commit to living that life. Unfortunately, if that belief is only intellectual when they face the onslaught of daily challenges, they abandon those intellectual beliefs because of fear and engage in temporal survival. If that belief is spiritual, they face those challenges knowing that when they look to God for direction, He will provide for them.

One of the keys to achieving spiritual belief is to understand that we have two sets of eyes. We have our physical eyes, and we have spiritual eyes. What do I mean by this? Our physical eyes see through the lens of the temporal world. We judge everything we see from that perspective and determine if it is good or bad. When we see through our spiritual eyes, we see through the spiritual world. We don't judge it. We let God's spirit direct our decision as to how we are to perceive it.

We must understand that there are two sides to everything. There is a positive and a negative side. When we look at a situation through our physical eyes, fear is always present, and we tend to focus on the negative and worry about survival. However, when we see the situation through our spiritual eyes, fear does not become involved because we know that God will give us strength and guidance.

Please understand that a vast number of our fears are just a perception and are not an imminent danger. If there is an imminent danger, we will automatically react to avoid it. For example, if someone comes into your lane and will hit you head on you immediately react to avoid the collision. We'll explain this in deeper detail in the chapter on fear. When we see this situation through the prism of our spiritual eyes, God directs our actions to handle it. At the time that Darlene joined me at Ft. Sheridan, I was seeing everything through my physical eyes and the prism of fear, I perceived everything as a threat in some way.

After Nick and I were assigned together at Ft. Sheridan, and we were living together, Nick's insecurities began to show. He would get jealous of something that happened and would express his displeasure. Me? I was confused as all get out. I love this man and would never cheat on him. I was frustrated by his actions knowing I was being faithful to our relationship. When we had these issues, and unfortunately there were many, we would have our chats about what was going on. I had my own issues about not being loved enough and to be confronted with Nick's distrust was hard to deal with.

When we had these discussions, we agreed to use, "the say it and then revise it." What I mean is if what I said didn't make sense to him, then I would try and revise what I meant, and vice versa. Years later, we learned why Nick had these jealousy issues. It was because he saw everything through the prism of fear, a fear caused by what he considered betrayal caused by his mother's death, his high school sweetheart cheating, and then his first wife not only cheating but the humiliation of her cheating with his best friend. He also felt a sense of betrayal by the army when he was passed over for promotion or given a bad assignment. All these betrayals, especially by the women, had caused Nick pain, so much pain that he assumed I would follow the same pattern of betrayal by what I was going to do or was already doing.

My love for Nick, and my belief that God put us together, gave me the strength to hang in there. Even after we realized why Nick had the jealousy issue, it happened on rare occasions, and I would get mad because these infrequent actions were hurting me. Thankfully, we haven't had one of these issues for a long time now.

I never accused him of being unfaithful, and he had plenty of opportunities to do so since he traveled so much. He would tell me about the women who would make advances on him, and he was embarrassed by them. I recommended he show them my picture and say, "My wife thanks you for your interest, but he is mine." Considering I always had said I would not get involved with a married man, because if he could cheat on her, then he would cheat on me. Somehow, I just knew he would be faithful to me, and I would be faithful to him. There was no doubt in my mind that God joined us together and had a plan for each of us individually, and for us as a couple. It was many years later that we were shown that mission. We'll share it later.

Darlene is the strongest and most wonderful person I've ever known. What she just said is the absolute truth. Since the day we realized that God joined us, and we committed our undying love for each other I've been totally faithful and totally committed to our God centered relationship. What she said about the women who made advances toward me is so true, I'd show them her picture and say, "My wife thanks you for your interest, but I belong to her and her alone." After that I'd go to my room and call Darlene to tell her what happened and we'd both get a good laugh from it.

Trust is earned by actions and Darlene's actions repeatedly demonstrated that I could trust her. When I would go off on my tangent we would sit, and she would explain the truth and it would settle me down. Those talks went a long way to helping me build trust.

Chapter 16
Somewhere other than the night

Yes, I love country songs, in fact for many years I was honored to play in a country band. I find that country songs speak to life and share its ups and downs.

In December of 2022 Garth Brooks recorded Somewhere Other Than the Night. The message in the words to this song are a metaphor for what was going on in our lives. Here are some of the lyrics.

He could see the storm clouds rolling across the hill
He barely beat the rain in from the field
And between the back door slamming she heard him say
Damn this rain and damn this wasted day,
But she'd been waitin for this day for oh so long,
She was standin' in the kitchen with nothin' but her apron on
And in his disbelief, he stood and stared a while
When their eyes met, they both began to smile

Somewhere other than the night
She needs to hear I love you
*Somewhere other than the night to know you
    care*
She wants to know she's needed
She needs to be held tight
Somewhere other than the night

The words in this song refer to "her" and her need to feel loved and held tight. In our marriage, and in any long-lasting marriage, they must apply to both the husband and the wife. Truthfully, the love spouses give to each other must go deeper than a romantic feeling. The love we express to each other must be from God's spirit of love as He lives within us. Intellectual love and romantic love can easily be affected negatively, by actions, words spoken, or the challenges of life. However, spiritual love is unshakable, when it is impacted negatively, it motivates the decision and action of forgiveness. We'll do an entire chapter on forgiveness later. I must say here however, that it wasn't until I learned to truly forgive and was able to forgive all of those who had betrayed me, that my relationship with God became real to me, and my total unconditional trust in Him and in Darlene became a reality.

It is important to realize that there is a big difference between love and like. I have, on occasion, worked with couples who are preparing to get married. The first thing I do is to ask if they truly love each other and they both spend a lot of time affirming that fact. I then ask them, "Do you like each other?"

At this point, I can usually hear a pin drop as they are not sure how to answer. I then ask them each to make a list of things they like and things they don't particularly like about the other. When they bring that list back, we go over the dislikes. Each dislike will fit into one of three categories. It could be something that the other person didn't even realize they were doing and therefore can be corrected over time. It could be something that they can discuss and work through together. Finally, it could be a deal breaker.

Sadly, all too often, one of the parties never mentions what they dislike and believe that they can change that in the other person. Darlene and I can attest to the fact that that is a herculean task. Someone cannot be changed unless they are willing to change. Once that decision is made, we can then become a change agent and support the person's desire to make the change. Most of us fear change. Why? Simply because it means stepping into the unknown, which is one or our greatest fears. Change takes courage and perseverance. It is also a three-steps forward and two-steps back process. Change is a journey, not an event. The bottom line is both must agree that a change is necessary, and together they will commit to making it a reality.

Frankly, intellectual love will wax and wane under the pressure of everyday living. Spiritual love, on the other hand, is solid, but can be stressed under adverse conditions. One of the biggest things to accept is that as the marriage matures, so does love. When a marriage is new, we can hardly keep our hands off each other. We want to be together every minute, and we think of each other every minute of the day.

However, as the marriage matures, the love matures and the hot romantic feelings and the long sessions of intimacy fade to some level. The good news is that spiritual love does not fade, it embraces the change and becomes deeper. The love is now motivated by deeper feelings of caring and companionship.

When intellectual love fades, the chance of infidelity grows. By the time you have been married and loved each other for so long, and weathered so many storms together, and your spiritual love refuses to even consider the very thought of disloyalty.

As you progress into your senior years, the words of the wedding vows, "In sickness and in health," take on a brand-new meaning. Taking care of each other in your later years is a challenging task. Darlene and I both have health issues, and these issues have a stressful effect on us both mentally and physically. Our spiritual love, however, never wavers.

Our love is strong, but what is just as important is that we like each other and have a deep friendship. Of course, God is with us every minute and through His love and grace we willingly and gladly do whatever is needed to help each other, no matter how messy it can get, yes illness and chronic conditions can get messy. But everything we do for each other is a labor of love.

Chapter 17
Life and time march on

So now we were living together and working together and have gotten into a routine. It is at this point that the baggage we each bring to the marriage starts to show its ugly head. As my Christian coach said, "Now we see each other's warts."

The great news is that Darlene's deep relationship with God and deep belief in us gave her the strength to focus her energy on me rather than selfishly wanting the attention to be on her. On the other hand, I was, as I said earlier, morally bankrupt. I suffered jealousy, lack of trust, and a simmering anger. I still looked at the actions of others with suspicion. For many years my motto had been to trust no one and to do unto others before they can do unto you.

So, what was it that made it possible for Darlene to accomplish the herculean task of bringing me out of the darkness and into the light of a deep and meaningful love and a return to my childhood love and trust of God? It was two things really. First, when you have a deep relationship with God He will guide your life, give you guidance and strength to accomplish His will. Secondly, was my work first with the Special Forces counselor and second with my Christian

Psychologist, my coach. There was a third factor of which I was totally ignorant.

What was that factor? It was God working within me to strengthen my spirit. Always remember that God never gives up on us. He is constantly working to bring us to a better life. In my case, He was also working to show me His plan for me. You see, God has a plan for every one of us. He gave us the right of free choice, to make our decisions from the spirit of His love or Satan's spirit of fear. When our choices take us away from His path for us, He puts up roadblocks that force us to change direction.

In my case, my five senses were giving me positive thoughts and feelings, from Darlene's love, actions, and deep belief in our relationship. From coach, I was learning to change my perception of the world around me, and how to respond to the life changes I was experiencing. He constantly re-enforced the fact that God wants nothing but love and good things in our lives. We must remember that God does all things for good. Slowly, God's spirt of love within me began growing. As it did, it began converting the negative energy of Satan's fear to God's positive spirit of love. My center line in my spirit began to steadily move to the left. Remember, there are no confidences, everything that happens has a purpose. Let me give you one example of how He caused me to change my direction in life.

I did not make a conscious decision on that cold November morning in 1968 to go looking for a new direction in life. Joining the Army was never even a blip on my radar, in fact it scared the bejesus out of me. My desire was to get coffee, get warm, and get back to finding women to chase and another bottle of beer. It was no accident that the only office open in that federal building was an Army recruiting office; it was God's plan for me. There are many more of these examples that we'll share that have given Darlene and I direction in our lives.

You know the baggage I brought into our relationship, and as I said earlier, totally open and honest communication is a must in a truly God centered relationship. The problem, of course, other than the little I shared with Darlene in that motel room in October of 1980, I had a lot of garbage stored deeply in what I referred to earlier, as my vulnerability vault.

What is a vulnerability vault? It is that place in our mind we hide away all the things we don't want others to know about us because if they knew, we're afraid they would probably disown us. We expend enormous energy trying to protect those things. An example, of course, was the lie I talked about as to why I washed out of flight school.

Don't kid yourself, we all have them. All too often, even in strong marriages, both spouses withhold those fearful things. Sadly, that has a negative effect on the relationship. Especially when something slips out, that's not particularly good. Your spouse looks at you and asks, why am I just now hearing that? As Dezi Arnez would say, "You've got a lot of splainin' to do."

One of the things that neutralizes fear is trust. That is why you feel safe talking to your priest, pastor or a counselor. They provide a safe space where you aren't going to be ridiculed, looked down on, or ostracized for what you say. Because of her deep faith in God, and in me, she showed me that she could provide that safe space. Her trust in me was iron clad while mine was still growing.

We soon came to fully understand that a sound marriage rests on a three-legged stool. Those legs are love, trust, and respect. If any leg is missing or weak, there is work to be done. So at that point we began our tradition of having what we call our kitchen table conferences. The rules are that we sit across from each other, hands on the table and touching. Instead of attacking or blaming each other we discuss the issue and how to best handle it. Yes, there are times when the issue causes upset. When that happens, the offended person simply says, "I need a few minutes to process this." Again, the third party at the table is God. We often find ourselves saying a prayer for guidance.

Have you ever felt uneasy or disconcerted about something in your relationship that made you feel uncomfortable talking to your spouse? You know you need to, but don't know how to go about it. Be honest, we all have. Here is what we learned from my coach. When you feel this way go, to your spouse and say "I feel like I'm walking on eggshells. Do we need to have an air clearing?" This then triggers a kitchen table conference.

While we are on this subject. Let's address how do we fight or argue and not damage the relationship. We started arguing about who loves whom the most. When I first told coach this, he said that meant that we weren't discussing any real disagreements and that was not at all healthy. At the next session, Darlene went with me, and he taught us how to fight and argue. He cautioned us that the old cliché, sticks and stones will break my bones, but words will never hurt me is total BS. In fact, words are seriously damaging as they are personal attacks and can't be taken back.

Just how damaging, you may wonder? Here is an example. In my freshman year of high school, we were all required to try out for the choir. Mrs. Scovel, oh yes, I'll never forget her name, sat each of us down individually at the piano and had us sing a piece she picked out. When I finished, she scowled at me and said, "That was the most awful thing I ever heard, do the world a favor and never sing in public." I took her at her word and never sang in public, until I joined a local country band many years later.

You've read about Darlene's childhood and how she was always made fun of and dismissed, leaving her feeling unloved and unimportant. The result was that she spent a lot of time and energy trying desperately to find love. Like myself, the words to the Johnny Lee song, <u>Looking for Love,</u> described her situation as well. Here are those lyrics.

I was lookin' for love in all the wrong places
Lookin' for love in too many faces
Searchin' their eyes
Lookin' for traces of what I'm dreaming of
Hoping to find a friend and a lover
I'll bless the day I discover another heart
Lookin' for love

I was in the tenth grade when I experienced my "first love". I have no clue why I did what I did, but one day DF walked from his home to mine. I was home alone, but I hid when he rang the doorbell. He left after a few minutes and when he called me later, I lied about not being home when he came over. It was dumb of me to do, but I don't know why I did it. From then on, all the boyfriends I had were from another school. When I was a senior, I met a young man and thought he was going to be my husband. I anticipated him taking me to my senior prom, but he cancelled on me so he could take his former girlfriend to her prom. We broke up shortly thereafter, and he married his former girlfriend. For me, it was a lucky escape.

Here is a positive example of the power of words. In my sophomore, junior, and senior years of high school, I took a class in speech and drama from Mrs. Horine, yes, I remember her name also. From the start, she told me I had a great voice and was a really good speaker and that someday I'd probably be a professional speaker. You guessed it, from 1990 until 2010 I was a professional speaker and earned the National Speakers Association's (NSA) highest earned award Certified Speaking Professional (CSP). Just like coach told us, words are powerful and deeply impact our lives. I'll wager you've got your own stories. What happens to us during those early years will affect our lives for the rest of our lives unless we take action to change it.

I hated school growing up. I felt like I didn't measure up because I was picked on or never picked to play. I felt disliked. I figured out years later where this came from. One year, my parents sent me to a summer camp for two weeks. Because I was so small, the counselor put me in with the kindergarten age kids versus the first graders, my age group. In my opinion, they stunted my development with kids my own age by putting me with children the same size, but younger. I felt the kids from my age group saw me as someone who was less than them because I was small for my age. I didn't get to learn how to deal with kids my age properly because I wasn't seen in the same way as the rest of my class.

After first grade, we moved to another city, and it is never easy being the new kid in class. Then we moved again after my sixth grade, and again, I was ostracized by the new class as not measuring up. This was ingrained in me and took a long time to get over it. Who would have thought that not being boarded with my age-appropriate class would cause me such harm for many years? Yes, what Nick said about the effect words have on us is so true. Fortunately, I was able to grow my self-confidence through my time in the army and then through my relationship with Nick.

So, here is what coach taught us about arguing and fighting. When you have a disagreement, never attack the person and don't make it personal. Always attack the action. That way, you do not diminish the other person, yet you are still able to discuss and handle the action.

Here is a funny, but valid personal example, from the time I separated from my second wife. I lived as a bachelor and picked up all the bad habits bachelors have, like leaving the toilet seat up. We'd been living together for several months, and I had been cautioned several times about that particular bad habit. Finally, one morning I left it up and this is what happened. Darlene came into the bathroom where I was shaving and said, "Sweetheart I love you dearly, but you had better stop leaving that toilet seat up or bad things could happen."

She didn't tell me I was stupid or uncaring, which would have been a personal attack on me, instead she attacked the action with a subtle warning about consequences. Please realize what I just explained was one of the spiritual messages Jesus sent from the cross. He asked His Father to forgive those for they know not what they do.

Chapter 18
Funny how time slips away

The song <u>Funny how time slips away</u> was written by Willie Nelson and originally recorded by Billy Walker. It has since been recorded by many different artists. Frankly, I think it probably applies to all of us. No question, we often say to ourselves, "Wow, where has the time gotten to? It seems like it was only yesterday that we got married and had our first baby. It was only yesterday that I held her in my arms and cuddled her tiny body to me. Today, I'm walking her down the aisle at her wedding. No wonder I'm starting to feel old." Here are the first two verses of that song.

Well, hello there
My, it's been a long, long time
How am I doing
Oh, I guess I'm doing fine
It's been so long now
And it seems now that it was only yesterday
Gee, ain't it funny how time slips away

Today, in 2025, Darlene and I are in our forty-fifth year together. It hardly seems possible. However, as we look back on our years together, we now have such a greater understanding and insight for how our lives have been guided by God. We now treasure the struggles because we learned from them and the wisdom God bestowed upon us. Over all those years and those struggles, with God's grace, His guidance, our love and perseverance, and our deep belief in Him, have only made our love, respect, and trust for each other much, much stronger. Our belief and trust in God have deepened in ways that are indescribable. We feel like we are still on our honeymoon.

What's interesting is when you are going through everyday struggles you don't necessarily realize that they have a purpose, or where they fit into the big scheme of life. What happens in our lives is, in fact, some way a part of God's plan for us. God is always with us working to guide us to his path for us. You only realize this when looking back. It's like the cliché, "We can't see the forest for the trees." As time slips by, what we learn from our experiences gives us wisdom.

As we grow older, God expects us to pass that wisdom on to the younger generations. Native Americans had it right They had tribal elders and a wise old chief. In our world today, sadly, that is not the case. But again, with God's guidance, we can correct that shortcoming in our society. I think the greatest way to show the power of the wisdom that elder folks have, and that is often poo pooed and considered outdated, is this story about two young Indian braves who wanted to embarrass the senior elder.

One brave told the other that he was going to capture a bird and hold it in his hand behind his back. He was then going to say to the elder, "In your wisdom, is the bird I hold alive or dead?" If the elder said the bird was dead, he would release it and let it fly away. If the elder said it was alive he would crush it and show the elder the dead bird. He believed his plan was fool proof.

As he stood before the elder and asked his question, the elder looked at him thoughtfully and said, "Young brave, the answer to that question lies in your hands." To me, this is a powerful example of wisdom.

Here is an example from the Bible, the story of Solomon's judgement. Two babies were born, one to each woman. One of the babies died and the mother whose baby died wanted the remaining baby. Solomon told the women he would cut the baby in half and give each of them half. When he said this the real mother immediately begged Solomon to give the baby to the other mother as she could not bear to have her baby killed. Solomon, in his wisdom, knew that the real mother would do anything to save her baby's life. With that he gave the baby to its real mother.

Chapter 19
A huge gift from God

In 1985, Darlene and I transferred from Recruiting Command Headquarters in Chicago, to the second recruiting brigade in Atlanta, GA. When I received my orders for the second recruiting brigade, we discovered there was no position there for Darlene. We were deeply disappointed and didn't want to be separated again. Fortunately, a position was created for her so we could be together. If you know anything about the military, positions that didn't exist don't magically appear out of nowhere. So, how did we end up together in the second brigade? It is quite a story on so many levels and shows how God's hand is always guiding our lives.

Here is that story. You may think it was just good luck, but Darlene and I see it completely differently. Earlier, I shared with you how I ended up in Boston, where I didn't want to be, and where I wasn't wanted and how one day, General Thurman showed up in my office telling me about my new assignment. My primary job on the Joint Optical Information Network (JOIN) team was to give briefings and demonstrations of the prototype system. By the time Darlene joined me at USAREC headquarters, I was making regular trips to the Pentagon to brief decision makers at all levels working our way to the final decision maker, the Secretary of the Army. By that I mean, full colonels and generals, from one star to four stars, members of the Armed Services Committee and under Secretaries of Defense. At one point I got to meet Casper Weinberger, the Secretary of Defense under President Regan. That first year I felt like I spent more time at the pentagon and up on Capitol hill, than I did at Ft. Sheridan. Finally, the day came to brief the Secretary of the Army to get the final decision on the implantation of the system's deployment into all recruiting stations and the Military Enlistment Processing Station (MEPS).

The agenda for the briefing started with General Thurman and Colonel Gregg briefing the Secretary on all the data gathered during beta testing and only, if necessary, for me to demonstrate the system. The night I left for D.C. to attend the briefing; I told Darlene that I was nervous because getting the approval was so important. Hundreds of thousands of dollars had been spent on systems development and a lot of careers depended on the system's approval. She hugged me, kissed me, and said "Don't worry sweetheart, you are really good at what you do, and you really shine when you're under pressure."

Let me explain the recruiting process. It is a two-step process: the recruiting station function accomplished by the field recruiters is the first part and then part two is the testing and physicals portion that is conducted by the MEPS. We had the demonstration on two floppy discs, one for each step of the process. Remember, this was in 1984, and computers were still in their infancy, everything was on floppy discs. However, for the Secretary's briefing we had put it all on one.

As I was setting up that morning, the IT specialist, who was handling the technical stuff, spilled coffee on the new floppy disc destroying it. When I asked him for the backup, he informed me he hadn't brought one. I then asked him for the most updated copy of the two floppies. Again, he said he didn't bring them. We were only forty-five minutes from the briefing with no software. I was in a near panic.

I dug through my briefcase and found two rather beat-up floppies. When I booted the first one, it worked. As I started to take it out and try the second one the tech stopped me saying the first one might not boot up again. Then I asked him what I should do if the second one wouldn't boot during the demonstration? His answer was, "Wing it sarge." At that point I said a prayer that the briefing by General Thurman would close the sale, and I would not be required to do a demonstration.

As the briefing began, I was standing in the back of the room praying that I would not be needed. There were fifteen people in the room and the lowest rank among them was a GS22. When the general finished his briefing, the Secretary slid back and said, "It looks good however, I'll never get the President to accept it as he only wants to spend money on boots and bullets. He doesn't like computers and doesn't even have a computer on his desk." At that point, General Thurman told the Secretary that he would like him to see the system demonstrated, and that Sergeant Nicholas would do the demonstration. My heart stopped, I could just see this failing and my career as well as a lot of others going up in flames.

As I started to move to the front of the room to do the demonstration, my heart was pounding a mile a minute, I suddenly remembered what Darlene said to me the night before. I now knew the ball was in my hands and the success or failure of the project rested solely in my hands. No pressure, right. I shook the Secretary's hand and began. As I started the recruiting station part of the process I felt a hand on my right shoulder. When it was time for the MEPS part of the process, I took the first floppy out and inserted the second one. You could feel the air being sucked out of the room and the hand on my shoulder squeezed harder. You see everyone in the room thought it was on one floppy, except the Secretary of course.

The second floppy was taking a long time to boot. I got nervous and said "Mr. Secretary, I've given a lot of these demonstrations, and I'm always asked if recruiters would be afraid of messing up the system as computers were so new. They couldn't hurt it," I told him as I started tapping on the keyboard and it was going beep, beep. "You shouldn't do this for too long though or a long hairy arm will come out of that disc slot and grab you by your throat." The instant the words were out of my mouth, I knew this was no place to make a wise ass remark.

Thank God, for at that moment, the second disc booted, and I finished the demonstration. As it booted, the hand on my shoulder went away. As I finished, the Secretary slid back and said, "You just got yourselves a system. You'll have your funding by December the seventh." He stood up, shook my hand, smiled and said, "Sarge don't let that hairy arm get hold of your throat."

After he left, the room broke out in cheers and back patting. I sat there sweating thinking, I did it, and it was all because of Darlene's loving and prophetic words from the night before. Yes, it was all guided by God's loving guidance. As we were leaving the room, the Colonel who did the briefing with General Thurman stopped me and asked if I was aware of the hand on my shoulder? I told him yes, and then he said it was General Thurman's hand, and when the second floppy booted, he turned to me and said, "We just bought ourselves a system. You don't need me anymore," and left the room. I guess I'll always wonder if this isn't what General Thurman foresaw happening when he came to my recruiting station that cold Monday morning.

As I prepared for my reassignment to Atlanta, we still didn't have a position for Darlene. It turned out that the Second Recruiting Brigade Commander was Colonel Viles, I had known him as a major when were both in the Kansas City recruiting battalion many years before. When he saw that I was being assigned there he called General Thurman and asked him to help find a position for Darlene. Later that day, her orders were being cut. I had forgotten that after the successful briefing to the Secretary. General Thurman had told me he owed me one and to choose it wisely. Again, there was no doubt in our minds that God orchestrated all of this.

Darlene and I have always worked as a team in every aspect of our lives, both professional and personal. Here is another example of that teamwork and God's guiding hand. In 1984, Darlene and I were called into the USAREC commanders office and told to go home and pack a bag as we were to fly out that evening to Washington D.C. to do a demonstration of the JOIN system for a political power group, Defense Advisory Committee On Women In the Services, DACOWITS. We got to the meeting the next morning and the IT specialist set up the equipment. Shortly after the members entered the room, and the Chairwomen introduced herself, she said there would be slight delay as the First Lady, Nancy Regan, wanted to attend the demonstration and she was currently in a meeting with Margret Thacher, the Prime Minister of England. Darlene and I looked at each other and wondered what the hell we had gotten ourselves into.

Finally, the Chairwoman said the First Lady would not be able to attend as her meeting had been extended. So, we began the demonstration. Darlene, who was in civilian clothes, portrayed a female applicant who wanted to jump out of airplanes, and I, as the recruiter, walked her through an interview using the JOIN videos to show her what to expect at the MEPS, in basic training, advanced training AIT, and at her selected duty assignment.

When we finished, Darlene left the room to get changed back into her uniform, while I answered the group's questions. When Darlene came back in uniform, the committee was astounded, not only that Darlene was on active duty, but that we were a married couple working together. Honestly, she stole their hearts.

Later that year, we were once again called into the CG's office and told to shut the door. He went on to tell explain that what he was about to tell us was classified. He told us that that morning he had received a call from President Regan's Chief of Staff, James Baker, asking him to pass a message to Darlene and me directly from the President. It seems that the President wanted to run for a second term but was not going to get support from the DACOWIS Committee. Their political power was crucial for his reelection. Our demonstration, and Darlene's actions with the committee members had convinced them to support his reelection and he was going to run again. We all know how that worked out. So, how did a farm kid from Kansas and a girl from Pennsylvania end up having such an impact on history? Simple, God has His hand in everything we do, and He has a plan for our lives. When we love and trust God, there is no limit to what we can accomplish.

Nick failed to mention why the JOIN project was so important. The Defense Secretary, Casper Weinberger's granddaughter saw the movie <u>Private Benjamin</u>, played by Goldie Hawn, and went to her granddad and told him the movie was so funny, and that the recruiter "lied" to Goldie Hawn's character. That lead Mr. Weinberger to order up the film's trailer and then ordering MG Thurman to, as he would say, "fix it."

So, I used that image of Goldie Hawn to play my part in the DACOWITS presentation. And yes, the movie is hysterical, even to this day. After Nick retired and started our own training and consulting company, Nick met Secretary Weinberger in the airport in Minneapolis, MN. He was on the way to Washington to testify before the committee on the Iran Contra scandal. He had to fly to Alanta and then on to D.C., so Nick had a real chance to talk to him. First, he confirmed the rumor we'd heard about why there was a JOIN project and much more. He told Nick that President Clinton wanted to put him in prison for the Iran Contra scandal. When Nick asked him about it, and he said that Clinton would never get him jailed as he had terminal cancer and only a few months to live. He laughed and said, "I'm going to beat the nasty SOB."

Even after we arrived at the second brigade, I was still suffering from PTSD and my suspicious nature, jealousy, and lack of trust was putting a lot of stress on our marriage. Once again however, God was there to guide our lives. I worked in the training division and one of our NCOs was having a lot of anxiety issues, so he was ordered to meet with a psychologist to work out his issues. When he came back from his first meeting he was really upset and said he would never go back.

I hadn't worked with any professional since I left Boston, so I got the name of the psychologist and made an appointment. As it turned out, he was a Christian Psychologist and over the next twelve years, I worked with him, and the result was astounding. I learned to manage my PTSD, since PTSD is basically an extreme level of fear resulting from a major traumatic event, combat, divorce, bankruptcy, job loss etc., you never get rid of it, you just learn to manage it so that it doesn't control your life.

As I went through the years working with my Christian coach, the strain on our marriage only increased. I was not the only one experiencing issues. So was Darlene. What happened to her is a statement to her strength and relationship with God. Since General Thurman was instrumental in getting her assignment, she was considered to have what the military refers to as political influence. Her situation was like mine in Boston. Her supervisor was a Master Sergeant who had never been anything but a paper pusher. He took personal offence toward her and made her life a living hell. Often, she was so upset it brought her to tears, at home, not at work. With my infantry background I wanted to invite him outside and rearrange his facial features and dental work. Yes, I am sometimes a hot head. She got mad at me saying that she was an NCO and didn't need me fixing her problems.

As I said earlier, when we are joined in marriage, we are joined as a couple, but we are still individuals and must honor the individualism of our spouse. Also, we as men, are by nature fixers. Our spouses don't always want us to fix a situation, they just want us to listen, give advice when asked for it, and support their efforts to solve the problem themselves. As men, that is counter to our DNA however, it is critical that we do this in a God centered marriage. We must realize that God is guiding us as a couple but also as individuals. We must consider ourselves as her sounding board, a place to vent, and be her unwavering supporter. What Darlene and I learned from my Christian coach had been so impactful towards the success for our God centered marriage.

There is no question in our minds that God put coach in our lives. Thank you, Harry, and thank you God.

What I went through during my second tour at the Second Recruiting Brigade was pure hell. My

116

first tour was Assistant Reserve Operations. The position that I was taking this time was that of Personnel NCO. They changed it from an E6 to an E7 position so I could fill it. I was a 71L Administrative Specialist put into a 75Z Personnel position. I needed to rely on the others in the personnel section to help me learn what I needed to do.

The supervisor did not assist me. No, he belittled me at every turn, sat right behind me and called me out for any mistake I made. He was destroying my self-confidence, but I persevered and did the best I could. I wanted to die I was so miserable. So, Nick stepped in and told me to stay home one day and unbeknownst to me went in and talked to the Major in charge of the Personnel section. He told him what was happening and when I returned to work the next day, my supervisor treated me like I was his long-lost friend.

Problem resolved right? Not even. He still nitpicked my work, but he was more devious in his actions toward me. I since found out that it was his *modus-operandi*. He would only pick on one female at a time, so it would be a "he said, she said" situation. I have proof of this though because at the end of my first year in personnel, my evaluation report was marked as excellent. However, after my second year, I was marked down in leadership capabilities and marked down for my physical capabilities.

Why do I claim this as proof? Nothing had changed from the year prior. I had a permanent profile which kept me from doing push-ups and do the walk vs. the run, so how could he downgrade me from the previous year? As to my leadership capabilities, he claimed my health issues were at fault. I left my assignment after I was diagnosed with Fibrositis or known today as Fibromyalgia. It is a stress driven disease, and the doctor explained that until I could get a handle on what was causing me the stress, it would not get better.

My supervisor was "my stress", and I don't understand why he had to be so nasty to me. As to why I had a permanent profile on male style push-ups, I didn't meet the standards of the soldier grading me, so I failed that event which landed me in remedial PT where all I did for five straight days was male style pushups. They didn't help me; they destroyed my body as I still suffer from shoulder issues to this day.

Chapter 20
What does being God Centered really mean

I'd like to share a story I heard many years ago about a man who lived in a village full of corruption, political unrest, fighting, and basically full of immorality. He was not happy, and he had a deep feeling that there had to be something better in life. One day, he heard of a peaceful land far away that was full of love, peace, compassion, and joy. He decided to leave his village of corruption and travel to this new land. He asked a couple of his friends if they would like to go with him. They declined, saying that it was too far away, and the road was full of dangers and passed through very rough and difficult terrain. Besides, they said, to finally get to the new land you needed to cross a wide, deep and raging river. No, they told him but asked him to please rethink this and stay here. We know that it is not the ideal place to be, but we are finding a way to exist and there are things that we can enjoy, even though some of those enjoyable opportunities may not be fully moral or even legal.

The man was very disappointed, in fact, even angry with his friends' attitude, lack of belief, and unwillingness to face major challenges to be able to live a loving, peaceful and joyful life. "I'm sorry you aren't willing to go with me but I'm still going."

They did all they could to discourage him, but he remained steadfast. "But aren't you afraid of what horrible things could happen?"

"Yes," he replied, "But deep in my heart I believe that whatever I face I will find a way to handle it. If it costs me my life, I deeply believe that I will then find myself in a far better place." Later, he forgave his friends as he realized that we do not all believe the same way, and even though he couldn't condone their actions, they were still his friends and were concerned about his welfare.

The next day he set off on his journey. Over many months and years, he encountered terrible setbacks, physical pain, and betrayal. But it always seemed that he found a way to survive them all. Oh, they didn't always come out the way he wished, but he survived and was able to continue. It wasn't all bad, of course, there were many pleasurable and happy times. There were times when after a terrible storm the sun would come out and warm him and make him smile.

As he traveled, he learned that if he started having negative or fearful thoughts, he would become depressed and consider giving up his journey. Then he realized that when he had positive and happy thoughts, his attitude changed giving him strength and deepened his resolve to reach that wonderful new land.

After many years of trials, tribulations, and betrayal, he came to the banks of the deep, wide raging river. It seemed this would be his most difficult challenge. At that point, he began to question whether he could cross that final barrier. He decided to sit under a large shade tree and consider the situation. He soon fell asleep. When he awoke, he felt stronger and refreshed. His attitude was again very positive.

As he pondered his situation he decided to explore the bank along the river. Shortly, he found a rowboat tied at the bank. He considered using it but then looked at how fast and swirling the waters were and decided to search further. After many hours of searching, he began to again be discouraged. Just as he was about to give up, he came across a foot bridge spanning the river. Unfortunately, it was in horrible condition and probably wasn't even safe.

He sat down to rest and to think. As he did, all the past years rolled across his mind. He saw in his mind's eye all the trials and tribulations he had faced and how he had found a way to survive them. Each time he survived one of these challenges, he became stronger and had learned new skills he could use as he faced other challenges. These experiences strengthened his belief that he could reach that wonderful new land. He then experienced a great epiphany. It became clear to him that when he encountered these challenges, he had tried to use his way to deal with them, but many times failed. It was in those time that he sat quietly and soon the answer to what to do came to him. He realized that that deep belief he had depended on was not caused by what he was doing but rather something much more powerful and stronger that came from deep within him.

A smile crossed his lips as he sat and listened to see if that inner power would again show him the way. Soon, he knew he needed to look further down the riverbank. Shortly, he came across a beautiful, covered bridge surrounded by the most beautiful light he had ever seen. He was drawn into that beautiful light and started across the bridge. He was now fully immersed in that beautiful light. As he stepped off the bridge, the light no longer surrounded him.

As he wandered around the land, he began to realize that it was not full of the peace, love, and joy that he had worked so hard to find. Sadly, it was just like the land he had left. He was disappointed and felt he had been betrayed one more time. But then as he sat and considered his situation, he realized that the beautiful light, which no longer engulfed him, was now in him and it had changed how he saw the land around him. He now understood that the land hadn't changed, but he had changed. He realized that the happiness, loving, peaceful, and joyful land he sought was not to be from the land, but rather it was already within him. That beautiful light he had entered now was centered in his heart. To make it even more powerful, not only had he found the love, peace, and joy he was seeking, he also realized he had gained great wisdom and understanding.

I believe that this story depicts our journey through life. It represents our desire to reach that place that we have come to know as the Kingdom of God. I also believe that we have a choice as to whether we live a life of misery, suspicion, jealousy, hate, and fear which is like a form of hell, or we can choose to live a life of love, peace, and joy which is like heaven on earth. Like the man in the story, even though we have been taught that God is our creator, and that he loves us, protects us, and tells us to never fear, we still, while we are young, have not fully come to understand how God guides and directs our lives and protects us from the slings and arrows of life.

The man in the story had always had God's presence at the center of his life, as we all do. However, just like us, he needed to travel life's journey to grow closer and closer to God until he reached the point that all decisions and actions are accomplished through the prism of God's loving spirit living within. By this I mean that God's love controls our spirit and gives us the strength to reject fears created by Satan's constant efforts to make his fear control our spirit.

Some of us, like myself, at some point completely turn our back on God and refuse to believe that He exists. Some even consider Him to be a myth dreamed up by religion to control us. Sadly, we live our lives in a level of misery that is driven by Satan's fear. Some, like I did, become Godless. Our actions are negative, hurtful, and malicious, even to the point of violence. People may even refer to us as being mean spirited.

The good news is that God is always there for us. He will reach out and help us to rise above fear and live restored lives. Of course, we cannot undo all the damage and misery we have caused however, our past does not need to dictate our future. Each day is a brand-new day with new opportunities. The past is past, let go of the past, through Jesus, God has forgiven all our past indiscretions. The future is a vision of wonderful opportunities and a joyful life, but it still is a vision, and it is yet to come, we must live in this day.

Be in the moment, make the most of each moment, we do not know what the next moment holds for us. What we learn in this moment and in this day is what prepares us to face what life holds for us tomorrow. There is a reason God only lets us see this moment and that is because we are not yet prepared to face the next moment, day, week, month, or year. We must let go of the past if we are to flourish in the minute and in the future.

Can you imagine a soldier collecting all of his/her worn out uniforms and other equipment and carrying it into today's battle? It would make it impossible for them to effectively function in the battle. Yet, this is what we do every day when we don't let go of the past.

The Bible tells us that God will never give us a load to carry greater than He gives us the strength to carry. Sadly, we often forget that He gives us the strength to carry today's load, not all the garbage from the past, that was already forgiven by Jesus' sacrifice on the cross. Each morning is a new day, the first day of the rest of our lives. It's bright and full of opportunity. Yesterday's transgressions have been forgiven by the blood Christ shed for our sins.

In the chapter on forgiveness, we will discuss this in greater detail. We live our lives one day at a time and God has given us the right to choose which road we take. Often, I've heard people say, it's just who I am. Not true, it is who you have chosen to be.

The young man in the story had a basic level of understanding of what it means to have God at the center of his life, but he needed to face the challenges of his journey to grow his strength, wisdom, and trust that God's spirit, living in his heart, would always guide and protect him. His new understanding enabled him to convert the negative energy of his spirit into the positive spirit of God's love and let him put his complete trust in God's spirit. That trust and deep belief led him to the understanding that it was not control of the temporal world that gave him lasting peace, it was his unshakeable trust and belief in God that blessed him with a constant great love, peace, and joy.

So, what were the key things that he learned on his journey that caused him to grow his spiritual relationship with God to where it gave him this new heavenly life he now was living here on earth? First, he learned that by forgiving his friends, he felt much better, it brightens our spirit. He realized that it was their actions, not them personally, that angered him. Then he learned that if he could keep his thoughts positive, his spirit was also positive, thus motivating more positive decisions. This was reenforced when he found the rowboat. He became discouraged, but his positive spirit motivated him to continue. He then found the walking bridge, but realizing it was not safe, he again felt defeated and became afraid that he would not be able to live in the new land. However, his inner power once again gave him hope, and he continued until he found the covered bridge and was drawn into its beautiful light. As he entered the light, he was overwhelmed with the knowledge that this was God's loving light and that what he had referred to as his inner power was, in fact God's spirit within him giving him strength and guidance. With that knowledge, he now deeply believed that no matter how hard things got, God would be there for him.

Not everyone is going to stand in the light because of a near death experience like I experienced. However, accepting Jesus as our lord and savior, and having the courage to let go of our false belief that we have control of our lives, and willingly turn control of our lives over to God, we will experience the same transformation and deep understanding as the young man did. It is when we reach this point that we are surrounded by the light of God's great love. Is it scary to have the faith to give control over to God? You better believe it is, but always remember, the Bible told us 365 times to not fear, for God is with us. You've got the courage to do this... don't let Satan's fear blind you to it.

To live in that beautiful and peaceful world here on earth, we must also learn to manage our spirit by learning to manage our thoughts. By learning to manage our thoughts, we in turn can manage our spirit of fear allowing the negative spiritual energy to be converted to God's energy of love. This deepens our relationship with God and the more of our spirit that is controlled by God's love. Like the young man in the story, we will face challenges, betrayal, and pain. But when we are committed to working at this and consistently pushing forward, we will eventually reach a point where we are transformed physically, mentally, and spiritually, because from that point on, our decisions and actions are directed by God's spirit of love. The Bible tells us this in 1 Corinthians 15:45-49, Paul's first letter to the Corinthians.

In the following chapters, we are going to share how we learned to manage fear and practice true forgiveness and how achieving this builds a deep trust that becomes the foundation for each of us. This puts God at the center of our lives, and in turn, puts God at the center of our marriage. When this happens, most of our decisions are directed by His spirit of love. Yes, we are still human and still make mistakes and make bad decisions. But again, this only makes us stronger and teaches us a lesson we needed to learn. Never beat yourself up for making a mistake. Mistakes are a necessary part of life. It is through mistakes that we learn and grow. That is one reason God gave us the right of free choice. He knew we would screw it up from time to time. However, when we blame ourselves, or others for a mistake, we only embolden our spirit of fear. When you make a mistake just say to yourself, "Well that didn't come out the way I expected. It's okay though because I did the best I could with the information I had at the time. Now I know more than I did when I made that decision. So, what did I learn that I need to know to achieve the outcome I wanted?"

Here is an example of what I mean. Imagine you are standing at the bottom of a mountain looking up at the top, which is your ultimate destination. From where you stand you see what looks like the best route. Later you look up again and realize that your first route did not take you the proper way. Now, however, you see the destination from a different perspective and can make a course correction. Was your first decision wrong, was it a mistake? No, it was the best decision you could make based on what you knew about the situation. Don't let this frighten you but an airplane flying from one coast to another is off course quite often and its computers are constantly making course corrections.

As you have seen in our story so far, in the beginning, only one of us was in the early stages of being God centered, and the other was a total non-believer. However, through God's Grace and with Darlene's love, strength, and support, I was able to regain and developed a very deep relationship with God, and it has completely changed my life and our lives. A priest once told me that my story seemed to parallel the story of Saul's conversion to Paul.

I have always believed in God, but Nick was a lost soul and needed help to get back to his beliefs and God assigned that mission to me. We learned later that Nick and I each had a forever mission and that those two separate missions were joined as one mission for us as a couple. More on that later. My journey, while it had been different and difficult, led me to Nick. As I worked to help Nick, my relationship with God grew stronger as well.

Chapter 21
Learning to grow our relationship with God

What we're going to share in this chapter, I have shared in my two previous books, Reclaiming my Life – My Journey Back to God, and My Life Reclaimed by the Grace of God, as well as with several different priests. Even though each one of the priests believed this was correct, they also said, "Nick, it can't be that simple."

My response was, "But it is. However, it is not easy." Yes, the process is simple, but it's the execution that is difficult. Unfortunately, it is difficult enough that many who try it don't give it the time to work, so they just stop trying and look for alternate solutions. Are there alternate solutions? Possibility, I suppose, but I've never found one as effective as this one, which I discovered in my journey back to God. Remember that anything worth having is worth working for, and there are no free lunches. Frankly, you will discover, as I have, that your journey to a deep relationship with God is a three-steps forward and two steps back process.

Many have asked me if it is so simple, why is it so hard? Consider it this way, when I was in the infantry and was involved in a field training exercise, there was always an aggressor force fighting against us. The same is true in everyday life. We work hard and strive to live a Godly life however, there is an aggressor force fighting against us. That force is Satan, and he uses fear as a weapon to blind us to God's love and direction, to keep us confused about which direction to turn and finally when the fear gets bad enough it paralyzes us. He also tricks us into doing things that are counter to God's commandments with his false information, false promises, and presenting himself as a wonderful and caring person. I'm willing to bet that each of us has met someone that we thought was attractive, smart, and loving only to find out later that the true person was manipulative, sarcastic, disrespectful, and often mean.

It is my opinion that we have never been taught an effective way to win the battle with fear which the Bible tells us is in fact not a battle of the flesh but rather a battle of the spirit, God's spirit of love versus Satan's spirit of fear. Yes, Satan is a part of our spirit and has been since Adam and Eve ate of the apple, which is why it is referred to as the original sin. This is not because those who taught us wanted to intentionally withhold the information, but because they didn't know about or fully understand the process. Please understand that we are not some geniuses that developed this process because we are so smart. No, we've learned it through our life experiences. Yes, I was blessed to be in God's beautiful light and Darlene wasn't, but it is through her closeness and involvement in my experience that she also has come to have a deeper understanding of God's actions. So, what we share we have learned and experienced together through God's loving guidance. Never underestimate or question God's involvement in your life.

We've shared how we learned of this process and how it has impacted our lives in such a positive way, in its healing power. Before going further, however, we would like to share what we truly hope to accomplish with this book.

I believe that the story in the Bible about the rich man and Lazarus best describes why Darlene and I believe what we share is so important. Of course, we have not physically died and asked to return to show others what we've learned in our journey to a life of love, peace, and joy. However, we have both experienced darkness, pain, and hardship, and through our experiences we have discovered the beautiful light of God's love, how it directs our lives and our marriage. Even though your journey will differ from ours, it will still lead you to the same place. The story I refer to is the story of the rich man and Lazarus and can be found in Luke 16:19-21. Here is the story.

"Now there was a rich man, and he habitually dressed in purple and fine linen, joyously living in splendor every day. And a poor man named Lazarus was laid at his gate, covered with sores, and longing to be fed with the crumbs which were falling from the rich man's table; besides, even the dogs were coming and licking his sores. Now the poor man died and was carried away by the angels to Abraham's bosom; and the rich man also died and was buried. In Hades he lifted up his eyes, being in torment, and saw Abraham far away and Lazarus in his bosom. And he cried out and said, 'Father Abraham, have mercy on me, and send Lazarus so that he may dip the tip of his finger in water and cool off my tongue, for I am in agony in this flame.' But Abraham said, 'Child, remember that during your life you received your good things, and likewise Lazarus bad things; but now he is being comforted here, and you are in agony. And besides all this, between us and you there is a great chasm fixed, so that those who wish to come over from here to you will not be able, and that no one may cross over from there to us.' And he said, 'Then I beg you, father, that you send him to my father's house— for I have five brothers—in order that he may warn them, so that they will not also come to this place of torment.' But Abraham "said, 'They have Moses and the Prophets; let them hear them.' But he said, 'No,

father Abraham, but if someone goes to them from the dead, they will repent!' But he said to him, 'If they do not listen to Moses and the Prophets, they will not be persuaded even if someone rises from the dead.'"

Let me interject something here. Everyone has a different opinion of what they read and encounter and that is fine as we are all as different as each snowflake that falls in winter. It appears we fall into one of three categories. Some will poo, poo the whole thing. Some will be skeptical and want to think about it and research it. Others will embrace it and begin to make changes to their lives. Regardless of which categories you are in, that's fine. We respect each of you and only wish God's blessing on you.

Okay, on with our story.

As Paul wrote in his first letter to the Corinthians, when we let God direct our lives giving Him our full trust and love, it will transform us physically, mentally, and spiritually. You read an example of this in the story of my hospitalization with the A-flu.

Our lives are controlled by our spirit. Every decision we make is directed by our spirit, either love or fear. Then of course all actions are directed by our decision. To live a God centered life we must ensure that it is God's spirit that directs our decisions. That is accomplished by learning to manage our fears, so the spirit of fear doesn't control our lives. As we shared earlier, our thoughts engage either our spirit of love, or the spirit of fear. Obviously, negative thoughts engage the spirit of fear while positive thoughts engage the spirit of love.

Why we need to manage our thoughts is easy to understand, but very hard to do. This is because we have an overwhelming number of thoughts every day which are generated by the information we gather from our senses. This means that everything we see, touch, taste, hear, or feel has two sides, positive and negative. It's the glass half full or half empty concept. The good news is that the more the spirit of love controls your spirit, the more probable that you will more often see the positive side of your thoughts. How then do you manage your thoughts so that you can grow your spirit of love and your relationship with God? Again, the process is simple, the execution is difficult. Let us share it with you.

Every waking moment of our lives we are faced with challenges. Here is another example. Another client that I've worked with now for many years, Andrew (yes, he gave permission to use his name), was experiencing a very difficult day when I met him for a coaching session. When I sat down, it was obvious that he was so upset that he was not going to be able to gain anything from our session. As he went into detail of the problems he was facing, I said, "Wait a minute, Andrew. Do me a favor and take several deep slow breaths." This, of course, helped to calm himself. I then asked him this question. "Can you think of an event in your life that made you feel so good that you wished everyday could be like that?"

He immediately said yes, and I asked him to share. Here is his story. He told me that he was French Canadian and speaks fluent French. He had taken his wife to France several months earlier and instead of being tourists, they spent their time immersed with the French people. They ended the vacation in Paris.

As he spoke, I could see his face light up, he became animated and couldn't stop smiling. When he finished, I said nothing. He looked at me and said, "What did you do to me?"

I smiled at him and said, "I did nothing, you did it; you changed your thoughts from negative to positive by reliving a very wonderful time in your life." You see, every event in our lives is stored as a full color video in our mind, and it has an emotional soundtrack, either positive or negative. When I triggered you, you immediately relived the event complete with your emotional reaction. The same thing is true of negative events. While you were telling that story you were not with me. You were back in France with you wife. Now, let's look at the problems you were struggling with, do they look different, can you see some possible positive solutions?"

He began seeing positive ways of solving the problems. His confidence in himself soared. He even went out and bought a small replica of the Eiffel Tower, which to this day is on his desk. Every time he finds himself thinking negatively, he looks at the Eiffel Tower and instantly becomes positive. Simple, yes, easy no. He had to practice becoming aware of his negative thinking because it takes work. We all find ourselves spending a lot of time thinking negatively because we are constantly being bombarded with daily challenges that we perceive as a threat to one of our instincts of survival, relationship, profession, financial, and the list goes on. I'm no different than you, I still experience the same negative thoughts, though probably not as many. My life event is our wedding. I'm standing at the altar looking down the aisle watching Darlene walk towards me on her father's arm. I'm immediately overwhelmed with love and can't stop smiling. Yes, I left you for a few minutes there and relived that wonderful moment.

My happy thoughts center on the day Nick gave me my engagement ring. He was visiting from

Boston, and that morning, when we woke up, Nick asked me to be his wife. I was so happy that we went to Service Merchandise and bought a ring that he could afford. It's not a big flashy ring, but a very simple one to show our love for each other.

Don't misunderstand me, there are times when fear is a good thing. If there is imminent danger to our welfare, such as a car jumping into our lane and coming at us head-on, fear will cause us to react, and we swing our car hard to avoid a collision. When the incident is over, we sit and let our heart rate and blood pressure return to normal. It is then that we must make a very important decision. How are we going to let this event affect the rest of our lives. If we look at it through the spirit of fear, we will probably decide not ever to put ourselves in this position ever again. That, of course, means you will probably never drive again. Or we look at through the spirit of God's love where we thank Him for saving you and drive on. This happened to me, and I felt such great fear that I refused to leave my house for over a year. Even after that, I would not drive without having someone with me. It took me many years to get past this traumatic decision.

This brings me to my story of my head-on car collision. It was Memorial Day weekend, and I was heading home when I saw a vehicle swerve into my lane and sideswipe a vehicle. I began applying the brakes and praying for him to recover. I felt it would not be in my best interest to swerve from my lane. Unfortunately, he did not recover, and we hit head-on. Ruined our plans for a great Memorial Day weekend, but at least we all survived the accident. My knees did get damaged in the accident and while I was at home recovering, I received a call asking me if I wanted to go to Saudi for a year. You see, I had just completed a three-month tour in Washington DC for Desert Storm, and they wanted to activate me again, but due to the damage to my knees, I was excused for being activated again. God's will that we were not separated again. I believe God has a reason for everything.

Let me summarize this. As you practice these techniques, that line in your heart that separates positive from negative, continues to move to the left and more and more of your spirit is controlled by God's love, and your relationship with Him grows stronger. Once you find yourself feeling positive, over sixty-five percent of the time you are living a God centered life. Can you increase that percentage? Yes, if you continue working at it, God will control more and more of your spirit and your life. Realize however, that this is a three step forward process and two steps back. You may ask doesn't He need to be controlling one hundred percent of my spirit for me to have a God centered life? Remember, both our negative and positive spirit are energy. Energy cannot be created nor destroyed. Mother Terresa, as spiritual as she was, always had at least five percent of her spirit controlled by Satan's fear and was capable of doing bad things. Hitler, as bad as he was, always had at least five percent of his spirit controlled by God's love and he was capable of doing good things. The only person to ever walk this earth, whose spirit was one hundred percent God's pure love, was Jesus.

Like the aggressor force we faced in our field training exercises, Satan's fear will fight back with something negative. Because of this, we must always be aware of how we are thinking, positively or negatively. Unfortunately, it is so easy to think negatively, as it has become our norm. As you start this process, it is necessary to keep a close focus on what your thoughts are until you reach a point where you develop the habit of thinking positively. This is accomplished by looking at each challenge that appears, trying to look for the positive side until it becomes second nature to always look for the positive in everything. Believe me, I don't care how dark the night is, there is always ambient light. Let me give you a personal example of how Satan fights.

After my book, <u>Reclaiming My Life -- My Journey Back to God</u> was published, Satan came for Darlene and me. For the next three years we experienced major medical challenges. Darlene has had multiple surgeries on her knees; I had four major abdominal surgeries and several heart procedures. Right after my book, <u>My Life Reclaimed by the Grace of God</u> was published, a dear friend called and told us that she knew Satan would come for us. She and her friends were starting prayer groups to pray for our safety. Will he come for us after this book is published? Probably. We, however, are not going to concern ourselves though because God always has and always will provide for us.

We've just given you a detailed explanation of how to strengthen your relationship with God. You may want to read it several times to completely understand it. In the meanwhile, let me sum it up for you in simpler terms. When your thoughts are positive, you are embracing God's love, and He is in control of your spirit. When you are thinking negatively, you are embracing Satan's fear, and Satan is in control of your spirit. Our thoughts are powerful, so we must monitor them closely.

Chapter 22
The role of forgiveness in a God centered life

I've got good news and bad news, which do you want first? I'll bet you've heard that before. Well let me give you the good news first. There is a part of your spirit that is permanently positive, permanently God's love. It's made up of all your positive experiences. The bad news is that a part of your spirit is permanently negative, permanently Satan's fear made up of all the negative things that have happened. Think about it this way, let's assume that twenty percent of your spirit is controlled by God's love and twenty percent of you spirit is controlled by Satan's fear. That leaves sixty percent undecided. It is your thoughts that will be the deciding factor as to which side is the winner. Granted, negative thinking will increase the negative spirit, but if it is followed by positive thinking, the negative spirit is converted back to positive. Unless, of course, the event that generated negative thinking is powerful enough that the negative becomes permanent.

Here is an example. Imagine that you discover that your supervisor is taking credit for all of your great ideas and then telling the company that he is the really smart employee. That type of event often will become permanently negative spirit. This is what happened to me. A series of betrayals turned a majority of my spirit to negative. By the time I met Darlene, Satan's fear controlled over eighty percent of my spirit.

Unfortunately, if we do not take steps to convert that negative spirit into God's spirit of love, our lives are a living hell. Believe me, I know, I've been there. So how do you go about making that conversion? One word, forgiveness. Only true spiritual forgiveness can convert your negative spirit to positive spirit. We've heard a lot about it from fellow Christians and from our religious leaders, but do we really know what it means or how to truly forgive those who transgress against us? My experience tells me the answer is no to both questions. I know I didn't have a clue what it really meant or how to achieve it until after my journey in the light. Don't be upset with your priests or pastors for this lack of understanding as they can only teach what they know.

I was blessed with many understandings after my time in His light. Let me share with you what I've come to understand about forgiveness and how to truly achieve it. Believe me, once you experience this, your spirit will brighten, and your attitude will change, and you will experience a completely different outlook on life.

As Jesus hung on the cross looking out at those who tortured, scourged and beat him nearly to death, you would think He would be angry and thinking of revenge.

However, what did He do? He said to God, "Father, forgive them for they know not what they do." Is this something you could do for all of those who have betrayed, abused, and taken advantage of you? I know I couldn't until my near-death experience. Since that event, I've come to understand many things about forgiveness.

What is the message Jesus sent from the crucifixion? There is no question, Jesus died to absolve us of our sins, but that is only a portion of the real message. Consider this, in His actions, Jesus told us that no matter how egregiously we have been betrayed, we must forgive the individual. Secondly, in His request for God to forgive them, he told us we must separate the individual from the action. Forgiveness is for us and for the individual, not for the action. Forgiving someone for a horrible action is not condoning the action, it is forgiving the actor. Frankly, most of the time the betrayer is basically unaware of what their actions have caused. If you confront them, they will likely look at you in confusion. Granted there are those who intentionally try to hurt people. In those cases, forgiveness is totally for you so you can change your spirit.

Here is a personal example. For many years after my divorce from my first wife, I still could not forgive her, or my friend, for betraying me. Finally, after many years, I forgave her and then Darlene and I befriended her and her husband. Unfortunately, every time I thought of her, I still felt low level anger. Later, she passed away from pancreatic cancer. The day before she passed, she called me at work and asked me if I still loved her. Wow, how do I answer that question? I told her that she would always hold a place in my heart.

Her reply floored me. She said, "I never stopped loving you and I will die still loving you. I did, however, lose respect for you." As I hung up the phone, I sat there stunned. The next day I got the call that she had passed.

Many years later, as I came to understand what true forgiveness was and how to achieve it, I truly forgave her. I've learned that first forgiveness is for us as it converts that negative spirit to a positive spirit. Secondly, I've learned that there are two types of forgiveness, intellectual and spiritual. Let me explain. If you do something that upsets me, being a Christian, I'll say I forgive you. By saying this, I believe I've forgiven you.

Unfortunately, every time someone brings up your name, I relive your transgression and become angry all over again. True forgiveness is spiritual. This means that I remove the emotional/spiritual soundtrack to your video. Once I've removed the emotion/spirit from the video I'm no longer affected by the event. When your name comes up, I may still see the video, but it will have no effect on me. That is what we mean when we say I'll forgive you, but I'll never forget. This is because the video is permanently in our mind. So how do you give someone spiritual forgiveness and what part does forgiveness play in a God centered marriage?

First let me share what I've learned about achieving spiritual forgiveness. Spiritual forgiveness can only happen when the video of the event no longer generates an emotional/spiritual response. There are many ways to do that, many of which require the help of a professional psychologist, psychiatrist, or some other licensed therapist. My Christian coach taught me one that I could do myself and it is not only simple, but also powerful and effective. He used one of my issues to demonstrate this before he explained it to me. He had me write a letter to my mother, putting my feelings on paper, and then reading the letter aloud, including my signature.

I've shared this process with many of my clients over the years and each of them experienced positive changes in their lives. I must say, however, that it can be very traumatic, as it was with me, so I make sure that the person is ready to handle the experience. Should you choose to try this, it is a good idea to have a neutral party that you have complete trust in with you when you read the letter.

When I got home from work the day that Nick had read his letter to his coach, he was sitting on the floor in front of the loveseat, and I thought he looked kind of dazed. He told me what happened and how it was suggested that the next time we went to Erie, KS, he read the letter to his mom's grave. I felt that that was too long to wait, so I had him get up and we drove to a local cemetery and looked for a headstone that said "Mother." He got out of the car and went over to the headstone and read his letter aloud. I'll let Nick tell you what happened then.

When we returned home, I was emotionally exhausted and immediately went to bed. The next morning, I awoke to the sound of birds singing, a light breeze coming through the window and the wonderful smell of fresh spring air. I felt light as a feather and the first words out of my mouth were, "Oh, my God this is the first day of the rest of my life. No one can ever take this away from me." For the first time in many, many years I felt a deep level of peace.

Now how does the ability to forgive impact a marriage? Let me share a doozy of a story I heard once. This couple had just gotten married and were on their honeymoon at the Grand Canyon. As they were taking the mule trip down into the canyon, her mule stumbled. She dismounted, grabbed a limb and hit it as hard as she could between the eyes. "That's strike one," she said. Shortly after that, the mule stumbled again. Again, she took the limb and hit it between the eyes. "That's strike two," she said. As they neared the bottom of the canyon, the poor mule stumbled for the third time. She dismounted, took a revolver from her back pocket and shot the mule dead. "That's strike three," she said. Then looking at her stunned husband she said, "Do you get my point, dear." It was obvious that forgiveness was not in her vocabulary, and she was not going to be willing to forgive her husband any mistake he ever made.

Thank goodness it is just a story. But the point is that we all make mistakes and cause others grief. But in a marriage, or any relationship to be long lasting and loving, we must learn to forgive. If we do not, this is what happens. Each time there is an argument or a major disagreement, a portion of the spirit is converted to negative energy. Sadly, there are situations where one party or the other just takes the transgressions and doesn't respond, but just holds on to their anger, as I did in the early years of our marriage. Then, one day something triggers them, and they let the other party have the full load of their anger and hard feelings. They don't attack the action; they blame the person for the action. Psychologists refer to this as brown bagging and can destroy a relationship. Thank God in our case I just said, "You piss me off," and Darlene laughed and said, "It's about time."

So, in a God centered marriage how do we handle those times when tempers flare and angry words are said? It is a combination of several things. First is that you and your spouse must be friends. It's amazing how it is always easier to forgive a friend than someone you don't like. Second, you and your spouse must like each other. As I said earlier, love can wax and wane but liking each other makes forgiveness much easier. Third, total open honest communication. When either of you do something to upset the other, do not let it set and stew. If you don't have time to sit down and openly discuss it at the moment, do as Darlene did when I kept leaving the toilet set up.

Sweetheart, I love you dearly but what you just did upsets me.

If there is more to the situation, then, when you have the time, sit down for a kitchen table conference and put all the cards on the table. Openly discuss why it happened and come to an agreed upon solution to prevent it from happening in the future. There will be times when one of you feels generally disconcerted and feels that there is something wrong. At these times say to your spouse, "I feel like I'm walking on eggshells, I think we need an air clearing." This then calls for a kitchen table conference.

Of course, when both of you have a strong relationship with God, this entire process is much easier. If the situation is extremely difficult, you should go somewhere quietly and write your feelings in a letter, sign it, and then read it aloud. In very extreme situations, seek out a good counselor and meet with them. Sounds like a lot of work, doesn't it? However, to have a long-term loving, marriage takes work. Remember, there are no free lunches. We have a choice, either to work on our relationship or lose it.

This is critical if we are to honor the words that were said in Matthew 19:6 *"What therefore God hath joined together, let no man put asunder."* Nothing in life that is worthwhile comes without working for it. Never take each other for granted and always consider your spouse when you make decisions that affect your marriage. A wise old man once told me, "Son, the best marital advice I can give you is this. Never let the sun set on and argument. Nighttime is for cuddling and loving, not brooding and arguing." To achieve this, we must work together and practice that which it takes to have a God centered marriage. Remember, practice makes perfect, but only when we practice perfection, and only God can give us what we need to do this.

Chapter 23
The mission

Think and Grow Rich by Napoleon Hill and The Power of Positive Thinking by Norman Vincent Peale are two classics that have remained popular over the years. If you've not read them, I strongly recommend that you do. Unfortunately, we often don't pay a lot of attention to our thoughts. Mostly, I guess there are so many of them and that we fail to realize it is our thoughts that determine our direction in life. Since there are so many of them, it seems our minds never stop processing the information it receives from our thoughts.

You may be asking, what does this have to do with our mission? It's simple really. Our mission is to help others to understand the beauty of, and the joy you will receive from having a God centered marriage. Thought control is the key to learning to become God centered and to achieve a God centered life and marriage.

I want to briefly summarize the process as we've outlined in this book. So, let's start at the end and work back.

1. All our actions are either negative or positive in some way. Are there shades of gray, sure, but one or the other will dominate.

2. All actions result from a decision motivated by our spirit, God's love (positive energy) or Satan's fear (negative energy).

3. Our thoughts generate either positive or negative feelings. All feelings are connected to either our spirit of love or our spirit of fear.

4. Our thoughts are created by information we receive from our five senses. That information is then processed by our mind based on a series of things including our experience.

5. Since our spirit is a vacuum, meaning it only contains God's love and Satan's fear, there is no empty space; meaning a positive thought causes a change in the control of our spirit as does a negative thought. Every portion of our spirit is, therefore, controlled by either love or fear. As we showed in our diagram, our spirit is distinctly divided between the two. Therefore, when we experience a positive thought, we experience a positive feeling. That feeling is connected directly to our spirit of love. It then converts some of the negative spiritual energy into positive spiritual energy.

6. Since our positive spiritual energy is God's love, the key to being God centered is to keep our thoughts as consistently positive as possible so that our spirit is continuously controlled by God's love and, therefore,

making our decisions positive. This means that our actions are also positive.

7. This is very important because when God's spirit is controlling our decisions, it is much easier to see things in a positive light, and we find ourselves looking for what's good in all things. Yes, there is both a good and a bad side to everything. Frankly, when we are positive in our thinking, it is much easier to forgive, and each time we truly forgive, more of our spirit is converted to God's love. The good news is that as your spirit grows more positive you will reach a point where you do not worry about what the world is doing because you are now living in true peace.

8. This may seem to be an oversimplification, but it is proven that people with a positive attitude go further in life and are much happier than those who have a negative attitude. The real reward, however, is that you are now much closer to God and your journey to living in God's kingdom is much, much brighter.

Darlene and I pray that what you've read here will, in some way, help you to have a stronger and happier marriage, and to live your lives in the sustained peace that only God can offer.

May God bless you with love, peace and joy.

Epilogue

As we've shared our story with others, many have said, "It is a wonderful story, but we haven't been in the military, had PTSD, or stood in the light. I guess, since we haven't done any of those things, and since we didn't experience the same shocks that you experienced when you first sat together, that means that our marriage can never become a God centered marriage as you have shared."

That is not true at all.

Remember, we all take a different to path in our journey to a relationship with God, and in our lives and our marriages. That path is determined by the events that happen in our lives and how we handle them. The first step in achieving a God centered marriage, is for each of you to build your own relationship with God. In our case, as you read, Darlene already had that relationship, but I didn't. For me to build my relationship with God required two things. First, I had to decide and commit to doing what was necessary to achieve that relationship, and secondly, that Darlene was committed and willing to be my support in all that I had to go through to achieve that goal.

The key to putting God at the center of our lives and our marriage is learning to control our thoughts and learning to manage fear. We have shared how to accomplish that in this book. Remember, when you manage the spirit of fear, God's spirit of love fills your heart. Use what we shared in this book to work as a team to build a strong personal relationship with God. This will lay the foundation for your marriage to become God centered.

Use the techniques we've shared in learning how to best handle the challenges that you face as individuals and as a couple. Remember, it is important to like, respect, trust, and love each other. Most of all, always have totally open and honest communication. Secrets create doubt and suspicion which is what Satan's fear will use to destroy the foundation of your marriage.

We've heard it said that there is nothing worse than a bad marriage and nothing better than a good one. I've been on both sides of that coin, and I can guarantee you it is true. I can also guarantee you that the effort you put into building a God centered marriage is well worth it, the reward is fantastic. Always remember, God wants you to have a wonderful marriage, but He knows you must work for it. Success will happen when you let Him guide you there.

So, as you as you begin your journey, sit together, hold hands and simply say, "God, we want You to be at the center of our lives and our marriage. Please open our eyes and hearts and show us the path that You want us to take." Then sit quietly and listen for His guidance.

I know we don't have the market cornered on a God Centered Marriage. I know quite a few people that have wonderful marriages, they just haven't written their stories down to share like Nick and I have done. We shared our perspective and journey to help people improve their chances of having a happy life with the person they believe to be "the one." I truly hope that our story resonates with those who need to hear it to help them become successful in their married life.

May God bless you all for reading out journey.

Testimonials

"If you're looking for a book that will have a positive outcome, then look no further. Nick & Darlene have opened their relationship to help others have a stronger and happier marriage with God being their teacher.

"I loved all of Nick's life examples of how God changed his direction in life and led him to Darlene... a union of marriage. A marriage where honest and open communications are the first steps to a successful marriage. A marriage of highs and lows but with God's guidance, hard work, support, and love."
Vickey Quasebarth

"In a God centered marriage you didn't just share advice; you shared your heart and in doing so you spoke to others. Thank you for reminding me that when God is at the center everything else falls into place."
Makayla Gorman

"I finished your book; it is so excellent. It will be very helpful to anyone in their marriage or long-term relationship."
Jill McDonald

"What a wonderful book. It was so interesting. We have been married for over sixty years, and you spoke to so many of the things that have made our marriage so great. The biggest was open honest communication. There must be no secrets."
Larry and Bev Simmons

"A very well written book by Darlene and Nick which explains how they have managed through many difficult experiences.

"While reading this book, I recalled instances in my past whereby I could have, and should have, solved an issue with less anger, more faith, and much better communications.

"This book will keep you wanting to read further to see how their next challenge would be solved with positive results."
Kyle Quasebarth